THE FABRIC OF KNOWLEDGE

THE FABRIC OF KNOWLEDGE

a study of the relations between ideas

J. L. JOLLEY

Contemplate the formative principles
of things bare of their coverings

The Meditations of Marcus Aurelius
book 12 paragraph 8

BOOKS
10 East 53d St., New York 10022
(a division of Harper & Row Publishers, Inc.)

Published In The U.S.A. 1973 by
HARPER & ROW PUBLISHERS, INC.
BARNES & NOBLE IMPORT DIVISION

© 1973 J.L. Jolley

ISBN 06 493365 2

Typesetting by Specialised Offset Services Ltd, Liverpool
Printed by Unwin Brothers Limited, Old Woking, Surrey

Contents

Foreword

The classification of the elements of knowledge is largely the province of the librarian and the specialist in document-ation, with help from the teacher and the linguist. Such people have sometimes developed a tendency to avoid one of the subjects they must classify, namely arithmetic and the more advanced mathematics built upon it. This attitude is not unreasonable in the light of the forbidding methods of teaching the subject to which they may have been exposed at school. Fortunately, matters are improving fast; but mean-while to present a classification based on a simple and easily memorised pattern is safe only so long as no one hints that the pattern may be related to mathematics and its fellow studies.

Yet at bottom the classifier and the mathematician are doing the same thing, finding and manipulating patterns. When I saw this book in draft my reaction was one of great pleasure at the pattern it put forward, and this was increased because the approach to my own subject came, as it were, from the side of the arts. It was a way to arrange ideas which arose from the notions used in everyday life, essayed the development of readily-followed rules, and almost as a by-product revealed a scheme for classifying the concepts of mathematics and using them as a means of ordering the other sciences.

I hope that one day Mr Jolley will turn his argument round, present it in the form of a hierarchy derived from mathematics and then test its applicability to the rest of knowledge. It has become clear that a systematic application of such a hierarchy is not only a valuable classification scheme but serves as a genuine research tool and an effective teaching aid. The advantages to research are gained from the way that a regular pattern reveals gaps where, if the pattern is consistent, something new ought to be found. The teaching advantages spring from the way a suitable framework makes things fit together, so that connections between ideas are easy to memorise.

One way of judging the value of a book is to see how much

further work it suggests. There is a great deal to be done in the present field of study; but Mr Jolley has made the main lines clear. His range includes the social sciences, economics, politics and management, but perhaps I may be forgiven if I deal for a moment with my own subject. The non-mathematician may skip the next few sentences, in the knowledge that his or her special study is equally recondite, in its own way, though it will seem easy to those familiar with it.

The order and system that Mr Jolley brings to the modern world of mathematics (specially algebra and analysis) is quite striking. It would not be true to say that there was previously chaos here, but the most avowedly systematic account, say by the Bourbaki school, is of an unsatisfactory nature. A starting point for Bourbaki is what is known as a set, a collection of things of any sort whatever. Bourbaki defines structures within and between sets in such a way that the result is mathematics as we know it. But why does he choose to define these structures and not others? There seems to be no inner motivation: the object is simply to impose a pattern that will produce the desired result. By contrast, an arrangement such as that here presented supplies a motive: an order of definition appears, based on the observed properties of the structures themselves, and implies that these are the structures out of which the subject we know exfoliates.

A good pattern, like that of the periodic table, must make its own way in the world. It invites attempts to prove it mistaken, to question its assumptions, to show that its gaps are blemishes and not merely undiscovered country. No doubt, faced with the considerable novelty in these pages, the reader will be tempted (fairly, I hope) to test their claims. There is always the question of how much reserve should be accorded to a view when it may be mistaken but, equally, may just be unfamiliar. There is much here which is novel, not least the belief that a universal classification may at last be with us, whose rules are independent of the habits of the classifier. The pattern presents a considerable challenge: may the book inspire others to begin the large task that it delineates.

C.W. Kilmister
Professor of Mathematics
King's College, London.

Preface

The first two chapters of this book describe an inquiry into whether the elements of human knowledge may be arranged in an order which is not determined by personal opinion and which is capable of being verified independently by different people. It concludes that this is possible and describes a theory which may serve the purpose. This part of the book is based on a paper presented at the First Ottawa Conference on the Conceptual Basis of the Classification of Knowledge, which was held in October 1971. I wrote the paper during the summer of that year, using the results of work I had begun about twelve years earlier. Almost at the last moment I found myself unable to present it in person, and this task was undertaken at short notice by Robert Fairthorne, to whom I owe a considerable debt of gratitude.

The third chapter is a commentary, intended to supply a background to the theory, to compare my present views with those of others, and to suggest applications of the work to practical problems.

I should like to thank *ASLIB Proceedings* and *Classification Society Bulletin*, in whose pages some of the material here printed first appeared, and the organisers of the Ottawa Conference, without whose invitation much of this book would still be in the form of disorganised notes in trays on my study floor.

J.L.J.

I

The Arrangement of Ideas

Standpoint

I have been trying for fifteen years to find out how people think. I do not mean how nervous impulses travel about their brains, or how they reason, or whether they visualize, though all these are part of the problem — that part which is to do with methods and processes. My own concern has been with a different aspect of the matter: with the materials they use.

These materials are ideas, mental images or representations of what may (or at times may not) exist in the world about us. The questions I asked were, what sort of ideas exist, how can we classify them, and how can we be sure that none have been overlooked? I also wanted to know how simple ideas were assembled into the more complicated sort. I needed this knowledge for a highly practical purpose: I was concerned with a special type of information retrieval which relied for its effectiveness on the assembly of simple notions to form complicated descriptions. Systems of this sort demand that their users can put their hands on ideas when they want them for the construction work they have in mind. In consequence it is essential to find a helpful order for the notions they employ. Sometimes the alphabet will do; but this has its limitations. To start with, it arranges words, each with one or more ideas tagging after it, and the ideas take up a random arrangement which makes it impossible to find them if their attached words are unknown or forgotten. Consequently, other patterns are sought.

Most other patterns are equally arbitrary, based on the mere decision of an expert or a committee; but even so they are remarkably helpful, once they have been learned in outline. Any pattern is better than none. However, if it is possible to find an arrangement which is inherent in the ideas themselves, this should offer advantages far in excess of those provided by patterns imposed by any personal opinion. It seems clear that the development of a universal ordering of ideas must be based on a study of the notions we believe correspond to the contents of the real world about us. This inquiry must supply rules whereby the notions may be placed in positions which they cannot help but hold. So far as is possible, personal opinion must be ruled out as a reason for placement: the only help must be that which comes from a careful examination of the structure of the ideas themselves.

Such a scheme of notions will bear directly on linguistics, since it will be the image which speech must represent, and indeed may even turn out to be the so-called 'deep structure of language' — the external pattern our notions imitate and which must in its turn be symbolized by speech. It will also be relevant to other disciplines, which it will support much as the periodic table underlies chemistry. No doubt its gaps will always be more important than its areas of completeness, for they will correspond to those places where research is still to be done. It will have especial value for those whose work is to catalogue and to classify what we currently know. The documents they index and file deal with topics which have a place in it, and the retrieval systems they create will be the more efficient for being more closely moulded to it.

I suspect that a most-exact model of this type will also display great economy and coherence of pattern, so that it may be of considerable use in the field of education. It is likely to set the major subjects of the school and college curriculum in an obvious, understandable, sensible relationship to each other, so that the bewildered scholar may the more readily see where his studies fit in the vast field of knowledge offered to him. This is consistent with the recent trend towards emphasizing the unity of knowledge as opposed to the differences between the traditional main subjects of school curricula.

So much for my standpoint, except for this: exploration and adjustment of such a pattern may never be completed, but I think we now know enough to get the outline right. It is to this matter that this book is directed.

A history of an experiment

My concern with this problem started in 1959. It was a spare-time affair, much interrupted, and it comprised three stages. During the first, which lasted for several years, I examined ideas taken from large numbers of classifications and word lists which I encountered in my daily life as an indexing consultant. My aim was to find what major varieties of idea could be distinguished, starting with as few opinions on the matter as possible, and consequently treating all other writings on the subject with reserve. I took no steps to avoid other peoples' opinions when they came my way, but I did not carry out a literature search or sit at the feet of any teacher. Indeed, it was some time before I realized I had embarked on any special voyage of discovery; when I did so, I was well on my journey. When the true position dawned on me, it seemed better to go forward than to return to find some charts of the unknown seas. I think this choice was right. Most of the arrangements of knowledge which I met in daily life were no more relevant to my needs than the doctrine of signatures is to the classification of plants. I had to start as innocently as I could, and to compare results with those of other workers when results were to hand. I decided it would in any case be a worth-while experiment to go where the subject took me, and then, at a suitable moment, to see how well my experience agreed with that of others. Later, I read extensively in the field of the classification of ideas, and found I was part of a great stream of effort and speculation whose headwaters were lost in the past. Fortunately, I did not then find anything which made me feel my results had been reached before. This was indeed good luck: I would very seldom recommend that a study should begin like mine, without a full survey of existing views: the chance of spending years doing work which is already done is far too great.

The outcome of this period was a general pattern which appeared to be complete, repetitive and internally consistent; but it was based entirely on observation and cried out for a formal theory, for mathematical underpinning. The second stage of my inquiry began with a search for this. Quite suddenly, in 1965, I realized that set theory provided the pattern I sought. I fastened on this and worked upon it, referring back and forth between the textbooks and my observations, trying to develop a simple, understandable terminology with which to talk of what I was about. As my confidence grew, I began at last to read the history of the matter, and to relate other people's views to my own experience.

By 1967 I was satisfied with the formalism, and the present stage could start. This is concerned with consolidation, drawing conclusions, finding applications and developing rules of the sort which may one day grace a textbook on holothemics, by which is meant the study of the whole set of notions we may form. Typical rules are concerned with finding the position occupied by an idea within the general pattern. Such rules can be reduced to a series of choices between alternatives which come in pairs and are mutually exclusive. Consequently they can generate series of binary digits, which may fit well in the memory of a computer. This property may have a special appeal for those who are concerned with handling information by electronic means.

Rules of this sort place ideas according to five main

categories. These are concerned with each notion's perception class, integrative level, formative rank and grade, and semantic type. Class, level, rank, grade and type may now be described — first briefly, as more or less bald assertion, and then in greater detail.

The general pattern of ideas

The concept of a perception class provides the first and most general distinction between the various types of notion we may form. It is based on the difference between the plain ordinary certainties of the world, which are accepted quite generally, and ideas which are held by at least one large group of sane people to correspond to no reality, or whose correspondence with reality is unproven or agreed to be non-existent. These are special ideas, which may be known to be fantasy, or may be hypotheses awaiting proof, or may be unprovable though many people assert them to be true. This sort of speciality has nothing to do with abstraction. Numbers are abstract, but they are universally held to exist, none the less. They are not doubted or denied as one might doubt or deny the existence of the Great God Thor. By contrast, religious beliefs are special. Believers may be sure they are true, but there are also unbelievers. The proper way to accommodate both is to give a special status to faith, making it quite distinct from hypothesis and fiction, yet none the less to do with how we interpret the world, how we gain special views of it.

Thus two classes of notions may be distinguished: the mundane, which is lower, and the special, which is higher, containing ideas which are often achieved by our imagination working upon and seeking insight into the lower. The main pattern of ideas with which this book is concerned is the lower. It is this lower, mundane, class which most readily displays the other categories mentioned above: those of level, rank, grade and type. These categories are to do with construction, with internal state or structure. For example, an integrative level may be defined as a consecutive sequence of sixteen degrees of complexity.

By contrast with perception classes, of which (on the definition above) there are only two, integrative levels are fairly numerous. Eight can be defined, each being well known as the province of one or more major sciences. As a result, three choices are needed in order to place an idea in its level. Fortunately, these generally appear in the guise of a single choice between eight alternatives. Thus there is a level concerned with atoms and molecules, and no laborious decision procedure is needed to conclude that the concept of an acid radical appears there.

The formative grades are the sixteen degrees of complexity within each level. They are divided into two ranks, in each of which eight of the grades are found. Thus a level consists of eight grades which form its lower rank, and eight which form its higher. A single choice is needed in order to determine rank; three are needed to decide upon grade; in both cases the decisions are based on familiar properties of relations, which are dealt with later in this account. It is not surprising that the properties of relations are relevant in this context, for if ideas are to be given places in some array by means which are not arbitrary then they must be placed according to their nature, which arises from their internal construction. The relations between their parts are therefore of central importance. This is why mathematics, as the study of abstract structure, may be expected to have something fundamental to say about the formative ranks and grades.

Each formative grade contains examples of eight different types of notion, which are the semantic types whose existence has led languages to develop the different parts of speech — nouns, verbs, adjectives. An idea's type, like its level, is often obvious, but in difficult cases a routine of asking three questions may be called for, and in these cases the criteria used for decision may be felt to be very like those

FIGURE 1: A hierarchy showing the pattern of ideas as described opposite with numerals attached as explained later

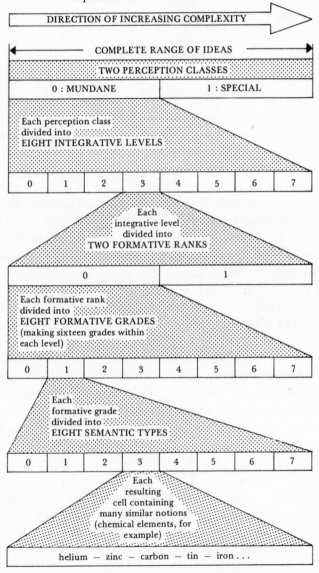

DIRECTION OF INCREASING COMPLEXITY

COMPLETE RANGE OF IDEAS

TWO PERCEPTION CLASSES

| 0 : MUNDANE | 1 : SPECIAL |

Each perception class divided into
EIGHT INTEGRATIVE LEVELS

| 0 | 1 | 2 | 3 | 4 | 5 | 6 | 7 |

Each integrative level divided into
TWO FORMATIVE RANKS

| 0 | 1 |

Each formative rank divided into
EIGHT FORMATIVE GRADES
(making sixteen grades within each level)

| 0 | 1 | 2 | 3 | 4 | 5 | 6 | 7 |

Each formative grade divided into
EIGHT SEMANTIC TYPES

| 0 | 1 | 2 | 3 | 4 | 5 | 6 | 7 |

Each resulting cell containing many similar notions (chemical elements, for example)

| helium — zinc — carbon — tin — iron . . . |

employed in grammar to determine a word's type according to the part it plays in expressing a train of thought.

These, then, are the categories of notion round which my inquiry suggested a structure of knowledge might be built.

Perception classes

To take things in due order, a more detailed treatment of the categories of notion must begin with a note on the perception classes as such, although the main emphasis of the work must be on the levels, grades and types which appear in them. Utopia, mallorn trees, Mr Bumble, the coming of the coquecigrues, phlogiston, Osiris, vital spirits, Ragnarok, these are examples of notions whose home is in the upper perception class. They are now generally accepted as fiction, even those which were once matters of faith, like the existence of Osiris, or of firmly held hypothesis, like the existence of vital spirits. Others, more important in this class, are the notions which are alive in the great world religions: redemption, the hereafter, reincarnation, the Church Triumphant. These, the concern of theology, I laid aside during my inquiry – at first unconsciously, and later in the belief that they might repeat, at a higher position, the patterns I encountered in more mundane affairs. In practice, I found myself beginning my task by contemplating notions of a sort I was later to call 'objects'. These were passive mundane entities with boundaries. Nations, plants and people are examples, and it is clear that notions of this sort appear in the special perception class also: Mr Bumble is modelled on a person, Utopia on a nation, mallorn trees on trees of our world of everyday.

As I grew to be aware of what I was doing, the distinction between special and mundane grew important to me, and it seemed useful to symbolize it. I made use of a binary notation, simply because there were only two choices. I allotted the numeral 0 to the mundane, and 1 to the special, with the result that the special appeared in the numerically later or higher position. Clearly, any further notation produced as a result of further inquiry, could remain within this framework. I thought of the entire set of notions we might form — the holotheme — as potentially suited to continued division of this sort, although I did not expect this division to be simple. I looked for great complexity, and indeed began by using an alphabetic notation on the ground that a mere ten numerals were unlikely to be enough. The persistent duality of things surprised me when I encountered it. This binary effect established itself during my examination of the passive entities of ordinary life, to which it is time to turn.

Chains of notions

The essential process in the study of integrative levels is that of making chains of ideas such that each earlier notion is a constructive part of each later concept, just as bricks may be part of a house. This is work which is fairly easy to do, if bounded material bodies — objects — are considered. I was fortunate to have selected these as the first sort of notion I would examine.

The following is a chain of objects:

> a proton
> an atomic nucleus
> a carbon atom
> a methyl group
> a phospholipid molecule
> a lipoprotein membrane
> a mitochondrion
> a muscle cell
> a muscle fibre
> a muscle
> a heart

　　　　　　　　a cardiovascular system
　　　　　　　　a human being
　　　　　　　　a degreasing section
　　　　　　　　a painting department
　　　　　　　　a production line
　　　　　　　　a factory
　　　　　　　　a neighbourhood
　　　　　　　　a town
　　　　　　　　a county
　　　　　　　　a nation
　　　　　　　　an alliance
　　　　　　　　the United Nations

It is interesting to form other chains and to compare them, setting similar notions together. For example, an electron might occupy the same line as a proton, and a plant cell might appear on the same line as an animal cell. When this is done, some chains will be found to have gaps in them; others will seem to have a superabundance of ideas. Here is a comparison of chains:

a carbon atom	a magnesium atom
a methyl group	.
a phospholipid molecule	a chlorophyll molecule
a lipoprotein membrane	.
a mitochondrion	a chloroplast
	a chloroplast layer
.	
a muscle cell	a leaf cell

It is clear that each chain calls for an expansion of the other.

When enough chains of this sort have been made, regularities appear. At intervals, the notions forming the basis of important disciplines occur: sub-atomic particles; atoms; molecules; organelles; cells; organs of the body; entire plants or animals; organized human groups; nations. This list is not complete, but it offers a starting point. At an early stage in my study, I named ideas of this sort 'units', and I wondered whether there was a general property by which they could always be recognized.

The answer, it seemed, was provided by the concept of homeostasis, as first applied in the field of biology. All the units possessed this property to a high degree: given favourable circumstances, they remained in balance with their surroundings. If not too severely damaged, they mended themselves. Even atoms, lacking electrons, trapped them if they could; and if a trade union lost its general secretary it appointed another. Units demanded completeness, and completeness appeared to be judged by degree of ability to survive.

However, from this point of view some units fared better than others. Molecules were more independent than atoms: they did not rush into partnership as readily as did atoms, although they too could interact. Cells were more independent than the organelles they contained, which mostly relied on the cells for survival. Leaves and flowers might die but the plant could still continue. An industrial company might close down a department, a state might extinguish old divisions, but the company and the state could both live on.

Integrative levels

I remember my surprise when I saw that the more and the less dependent units alternated along the entire length of any chain within which no units were omitted. This is the sort of regularity which encourages anyone looking for a pattern, because it appears without being forced, and justifies the procedure of simply gazing at one's problem in a questioning way.

My own first list of units ran as follows:

> photons
> PARTICLES (with rest mass)
> atoms
> MOLECULES

> organelles
> CELLS
> organs
> PLANTS AND ANIMALS
> departments
> COMMUNITIES
> local governments
> NATIONS

I noticed with interest that it was notably organic. It did not deal with artefacts, which I would have to examine later. Also, I observed a second pattern in the chain. Every fourth unit seemed in some way to be eminent, to be a culmination of the ideas which went before. The physical sciences aspired to molecules and molecular substances; the life sciences rose to the study of living beings; the social sciences culminated in the political, social and economic behaviour of nations and of their unions and alliances.

Such effects as this made it seem very much as if the underlying pattern was binary. If this was so, then it was hard to resist the view that a list containing twelve units was incomplete. There ought to be sixteen. The positions held by the remaining four might, of course, come after that held by nations; but this view had little to recommend it compared with the alternative, that they came before photons and were, in fact, to do with mathematics. I remembered reading speculations that physicists might one day have to make matter out of space, and I guessed that two units concerned with geometries might precede the photons and particles of sub-atomic physics, while two units of even greater simplicity occupied the two positions at the very start of the chain. I therefore added the following to my list:

> members of sets
> FULL SETS
> points
> LINES, LINEAR SPACES

This looked reasonable, if only because photons, which followed lines in my list, were described by means of lines — in fact, of sine waves. I had to make an adjustment to my rules, however: below the photon, I could not talk of objects being made out of simpler objects, but only of objects being described in terms of simpler objects. Yet, even here, I wondered whether colloquial speech was not wiser than my reasoning: even a child at school will cheerfully talk of a square being made out of lines.

And now yet another manifestation of a binary pattern appeared — this time employing the powers of two, namely one, two and four. If I divided my set of units in half, then life appeared at the start of the upper half, with organelles, after my fourth major unit. If I divided the lower half in two, then energy appeared at the start of the upper part of this division, with photons, after my second major unit. If I again divided the lower part in two, then space appeared at the start of the upper section of this division, with points, after my first major unit.

I drew a line after each major unit, thus making obvious the eight integrative levels, each containing such a unit — starting its upper rank, as I later found — preceded by a subunit. Each pair of levels was the domain of a majestic set of disciplines — in order, the mathematical, physical, life and social sciences. On an even larger scale, I gazed upon two kingdoms: four levels of inanimate notions, and four of living things.

Formative grades

In the early stages of the study I paid scant attention to mathematics, despite my conclusion that set theory and geometries occupied the two lowest levels. I was more concerned to discover what lay between one unit and the next, and this involved examining ideas from levels above the mathematical, which seemed a little too abstract for my

FIGURE 2: Some binary effects in the pattern of ideas, using octal and binary reference numbers for the levels as explained later. Note how occurring *in* level one means occurring *after* one level, and so *on*

octal level number	binary level number	major type of notion	first appearance of idea of	domain	
0	000	member SET		mathematical sciences (two levels)	Two domains of the INANIMATE KINGDOM
1 ($= 2^0$)	001	point SPACE	space (after *one* level)		
2 ($= 2^1$)	010	photon PARTICLE	energy (after *two* levels)	physical sciences (two levels)	
3	011	atom MOLECULE			
4 ($= 2^2$)	100	organelle CELL	life (after *four* levels)	life sciences (two levels)	Two domains of the ANIMATE KINGDOM
5	101	organ BEING			
6	110	department COMMUNITY		social sciences (two levels)	
7	111	local authority NATION			
special perception class begins after eight ($= 2^3$) levels of the mundane perception class					

purpose. I began by considering those ideas which came immediately after units in my chains. There was an immediate result: my collection of these contained a marked preponderance of what I called 'assemblies': groups of units in which no precedence could be found. The two electrons in the innermost orbit of an atom afford an example; so do the members of a leaderless group of people involved in a general discussion; so do a pair of eyes, the atoms in a hydrogen molecule; the sides of a hexagon, a pair of cufflinks, a swarm of midges, the voters in an election when each has one vote only.

The notions which followed assemblies also had something in common. Sequence, precedence, order appeared in them. Examples are afforded by a production line in a factory, the digestive system of an animal, the rainwater system of a house. I found the name 'system' was so frequently used in connection with them that for a time I adopted it; but in due course it began to seem better to emphasise the seriality of the collections of units involved, so I began to use the word 'series' for notions of this type.

When units, assemblies and series had been removed from my chains of ideas very little remained. That little, however, was of considerable interest. It consisted of reciprocal or interactive series (I thought of them as assemblies of series), and it introduced an effect of feedback. Examples are: the afferent and efferent nervous systems taken together (and generally, with the brain and the spinal cord, called the central nervous system); the transmission, ignition, braking and other systems, taken together, of a motor vehicle without its bodywork (I have often seen those driven past my window on their way from the engineer to the coachbuilder); the two series of unit parts which between them make two-way conversation possible by telephone. At first, after some hesitation, I called these reciprocal series 'combines'; but when unidirectional sequences had been named 'series' the word 'system' became free and I applied it to assemblies of series which displayed this internal balancing tendency. It chimed in well with current practice: general systems theory is concerned with interacting series. Notions of this sort are central to the study of cybernetics. It is hard to overrate their importance.

When sufficient series are brought together in this way, the resulting complex system is sufficiently interactive to produce a new unit, ensuring its homeostasis by the co-operation of its many trains of elements.

This method of examining ideas reveals four steps, including a lower unit, assembly, series and system, before a higher unit is reached, and since I had found two units, a major and a minor, in my integrative levels I concluded that each level contained eight steps of this sort. Of these, the first four led up from the lower unit to the unit which, being major, I thought of as central to the level; the second four led on to the lower unit of the next level upward. I found it helpful to think of these as formative stages, stages in the formation of higher things from lower. Soon each of these eight was to be divided in two, to form sixteen in all. Meanwhile I added a little to my terminology, calling a unit of a lower rank a subunit, an assembly of a lower rank a subassembly, and so on. With this convention, an atom became a molecular subunit and the alimentary canal of a human being became a subseries in the level of plants and animals.

To proceed, a new distinction must be called into play. As an immediate example, consider the difference between an atom of copper and copper as a substance. One is an object; the other is a large collection of such things, an idea without bounds, copper atoms on and on till we stop bothering to think about them, copper atoms to infinity. The same situation is found at other levels: electricity is a boundless collection of electrons, space can be thought of as a boundless collection of points, mist is a boundless collection of droplets, water a boundless collection of molecules of that substance, yeast a boundless collection of yeast plants. Further, not all substances are simple in the sense of being made of units of one sort only. Others are mixtures: air is an example. Yet others have an even more complex internal structure — consider plywood. In the case of plywood the substance is bounded in one dimension but no specific bounds are set in the other two.

There is a significant comparison to be drawn between units and assemblies, on the one side, and simples and mixtures, on the other. Units and assemblies are concerned with objects; simples and mixtures are concerned with substances. There is no necessary order about the internal structure of simples or mixtures; but if sheetlike or laminar substances are considered then an order can be made: in the case of three-ply plywood this may be: first ply — middle ply — last ply. Suppose that sheets are equated to series, accordingly: can we then find something which may be equated to systems? Sheets are bounded in one dimension: perhaps materials which are bounded in two dimensions might fill this higher role. Examples are afforded by hosepiping, rope, cinematograph film. These are of indeterminate length, but breadth and thickness are assumed. After trying various names for them, I ended by called them 'stretches'.

To take this to a conclusion: the next move should be to consider substances bounded in three dimensions. These, however, appeal to us directly as objects. They are clearly units, as indeed might be expected, since at this point on the upward path another rank (another lower or upper half-level) becomes available.

This line of argument led me to divide each formative stage into two, one part serving to accommodate objects and the other to accommodate substances. These parts I named 'grades', and it is from this division that the sixteen grades of each integrative level are derived: eight grades in each rank of the level.

FIGURE 3: The sequence of formative grades in any level, showing its binary pattern, with octal and binary notation as described later

	octal grade number	binary grade number	grade name	first appearance in level of
LOWER RANK	0.0	0.000	subunit	
	0.1	0.001	subsimple	boundlessness, infinity (after one grade)
	0.2	0.010	subassembly	reciprocity, symmetry (after two grades)
	0.3	0.011	submixture	
	0.4	0.100	subseries	order (after four grades)
	0.5	0.101	subsheet	
	0.6	0.110	subsystem	
	0.7	0.111	substretch	
UPPER RANK	1.0	1.000	unit	completion (of main unit) (after eight grades)
	1.1	1.001	simple	
	1.2	1.010	assembly	
	1.3	1.011	mixture	
	1.4	1.100	series	
	1.5	1.101	sheet	
	1.6	1.110	system	
	1.7	1.111	stretch	

In this table, reciprocity is shown as a property which first appears in subassemblies: it is to be thought of as a relationship between the things concerned (as one is to the other, so the other is to the one). In this sense, 'symmetry' is another name for it.

Note that the grade names are chosen with respect to objects and substances: other grade names may be more helpful for other types of idea.

Artefacts

Consideration of materials — wire, rubber and the like — led me to become concerned with the placing of artefacts in my chain of integrative levels. Books, cups and saucers, chairs, pianos, roofing tiles, bottles of weedkiller, the Venus de Milo, transistors, jet engines, football boots, electric shavers and battleships all required a home. It was a land of pitfalls. I knew, for example, that an idea was not more advanced than another idea simply because it physically contained that other idea: tortoises are contained in shells, but they are more advanced than the shells which contain them. Again, I knew that physical size was nothing to go by: the sun, for all its immensity, is not as advanced as a boll weevil. I suspected that a hinge, incorporating the facility of movement, might be higher than the door and door frame which it served to connect, however complex these might be, so long as they were rigid in themselves. Such things as hinges, scissors, locks, latches and the like I called 'adjustable devices'.

In the end I set up the hypothesis that the two levels between that of molecules and that of communities were occupied, on the mechanic side, by two pairs of units (with their appropriate assemblies, series and systems) as follows:

> single-piece parts
> ADJUSTABLE DEVICES
> engines and other organs of machines
> MACHINES

At the level of communities the two branches of the chain came together: a farm, for instance, consists not only of people, other animals and plants, but also of buildings, tractors and harvesting machinery.

After experimenting with more chains of ideas I concluded that this was satisfactory, though it seemed that unitary completeness could not be judged in the light of homeostasis on the mechanic side. Instead, it was something to do with fitness for purpose. None the less, I believed I could recognize a unit artefact when I saw one. My lawnmower ceased to be one when its handle broke away.

While I was looking at this part of the problem, I was met several times by the question 'Why, if tools and machines are inanimate, should they occupy levels which are mainly concerned with life?' There certainly seems to be a good common-sense argument for placing implements and machinery of all kinds at some inanimate physical level, moving off sideways, so to speak, from the main stem of the pattern as it rises through the grades. The argument which decided the matter for me may have been somewhat childlike: tools are extensions of the animal. A bicycle is an improved pair of legs, a pair of pliers is a hand with a stronger grip, a microscope is an improvement on the unaided power of the eye. A man with an implement is more effective than a man without. Artefacts are made because they are lifelike in this respect. They occupy the levels of life.

Notation for levels and grades

To proceed, the levels must be named and numbered. The following names and numbers, the latter in both octal and binary, may suit:

> 000 : level 0 : set-theoretic : members of sets, full sets
> 001 : level 1 : spatial : points, lines and linear spaces
> 010 : level 2 : subatomic : photons, massy particles such as electrons
> 011 : level 3 : molecular : atoms, molecules
> 100 : level 4 : cytomechanic : organelles, cells; and also single-piece parts, adjustable devices
> 101 : level 5 : biomorphic : organs, plants and animals: and also engines and organs of machines, machines
> 110 : level 6 : communal : departments, organisations
> 111 : level 7 : national : local governments, nations

This notation may be added to that for the perception

classes, placing the class first and interposing a point between the class and the level. Then, in binary, Utopia, Ruritania and other imaginary nations occur in a position whose code sequence (class and level) is 1.111. Canada, France and other real nations occur at position 0.111. Copper atoms are at 0.011. Ottawa University is at 0.110. In octal, these sequences are 1.7, 0.7, 0.3 and 0.6 respectively.

A code sequence for the formative ranks and grades may also be made, starting with a zero for the lower rank of a level and a unit for the upper. If a point is used to separate the level code sequence from the grade code sequence, then Canada and France, being main units at national level, will gain the sequence 0.111.1, signifying mundane, national level, upper rank. Cooper atoms, being subunits at molecular level, will gain sequence 0.011.0, meaning mundane, molecular level, lower rank. Within each rank, further notation may then be applied, as follows:

units	: 000	(relevant to objects)
simples	: 001	(relevant to substances)
assemblies	: 010	(relevant to objects)
mixtures	: 011	(relevant to substances)
series	: 100	(relevant to objects)
sheets	: 101	(relevant to substances)
systems	: 110	(relevant to objects)
stretches	: 111	(relevant to substances)

In this arrangement, the right-hand position of the code sequences holds a zero if the notion to which it refers concerns an object and a unit if it concerns a substance. In the middle position, the zero indicates a sort of singleness and the unit shows the condition of assembly or mixture — a system being an assembly of single series and a stretch being formed by a mixture or assembly of sheets forming an envelope. The way this may be interpreted at the higher levels of integration is still a matter for inquiry. The left-hand position carries a zero if order does not matter and a unit when order makes an appearance.

The code sequences for Canada, France, copper atoms and the like may now be extended further, completing the notation for formative degrees by adding triads to show the grades within the ranks. Again a point may be used, this time between rank and grade. Thus the two nations gain the sequence 0.111.1.000, the grade triad showing that they are units and the rank monad that they are in the upper part of a level. Atoms gain sequence 0.011.0.000, being units also, but in their level's lower rank. As a further example, the digestive tract is a biomorphic subseries and carries the code sequence 0.101.0.100, meaning mundane, biomorphic, (sub)series as required.

Again an octal expression is possible, each binary number, monad or triad, being converted to a numeral from 0 to 7. The nations then obtain sequence 0.7.1.0, which may be shortened to 0710 without loss of information. Atoms are numbered 0300; the digestive tract is allotted sequence 0504. These four-figure references give class, level, rank and grade in compact form.

Semantic types

The study of semantic types is not unlike that of integrative levels. Major varieties of notion are identified and set aside from a collection of ideas, type by type, until none remain. For this part of my inquiry I took words at random from a dictionary, laid aside all those which I recognized as referring to objects or substances, and looked carefully at the rest. It was almost too obvious that objects and substances, which I called collectively 'things', were both passive and entitive. Since the passive contrasts with the active, whilst the entitive may be set against the attributive, this suggested immediately that three other types of notion might be expected to exist. These would be respectively passive and attributive, active and entitive, and active and attributive. Here the use of contrasting pairs of properties offers yet another binary pattern.

There is little difficulty in applying this analysis. Passive attributive notions are easy to find: they are qualities, such as 'blue', 'triangular', 'cheap' and 'northern'. Active entities are also much in evidence, being phenomena like rain, wind, the battle of Salamis, a grand dance, a surprise. Active attributes describe phenomena just as those of the passive sort describe things. Since my daily work at the time I examined this problem was concerned with indexing such occurrences as sales, breakdowns, accidents and incidents, my files were full of examples. They dealt with when and how events occurred. The problem was not to find such notions but to decide upon what to call them. I could find no commonly accepted name for them. In the end I settled for the word 'mode'. An active entitive notion describes the mode of occurrence of a phenomenon.

I compared modes with qualities, and this led me to look again at many adjectives I had thought were to do with the properties of things. For example, in the phrase 'that factory is productive', the adjective 'productive' is not strictly descriptive of the factory, but of the phenomenon of manufacturing. Thus I learnt that the part of a word may play in speech is no sure guide to the type of notion it represents. It is only a general indication of this, though often a good one.

At this stage, almost all the words remaining in my list were verbs. It took me a long time to realize what I am sure others could have seen in a flash, namely that verbs represent a sort of idea which connects other ideas, that they are to do with relations. My readings in logic had made me familiar with the distinction between a term (adjectival or substantive) and a relation. Here I had a third dichotomy.

Introduction of relations

Thus at last I found myself concerned with the study of relations. Relations give structure to terms, whether the terms be modes, qualities, things or phenomena. Relations between simpler notions become relations within more complex notions. Each term is provided with its own variety of relation: passive entitive relations (like being-bent-round, being-contained-in and being-beside) inform things. Passive attributive relations give form to qualities. Active attributive relations are found in modes. Active entitive relations are embodied in phenomena: thus exploding, falling, running, encountering are the relations we meet in explosions, tumbles, races, meetings.

When I had set aside all the words in my collection which referred to one or other of the four types of term, or of the four types of relation, very little remained. This little comprised two interjections, the indefinite article, and a word of indeterminate meaning which occurs in a work by Shakespeare: honorificabilitudinitatibus. I decided that my set of semantic types was complete. However, names were still needed for those which were relations.

I did not find much help in the literature on the subject. The most widely agreed word in English was 'operations', a name which was applied to any relation of the active sort. In many textbooks on mathematics, passive relations were known simply as 'relations', the passivity being implied. For these I adopted the title 'conditions'. Then, after several trials with words whose other meanings often led me astray, I concluded that entitive conditions could well be called 'structures', whilst those of the attributive sort could be named 'states'. For entitive operations I used the word 'actions' and for attributive operations the title 'activities'.

Since binary code sequences can be allotted to classes, levels and grades, it is natural to consider allotting them to semantic types also. The three dichotomies provide a basis for this, the only problem being that of deciding upon an order of precedence for them. On the ground that all ideas embody relations, which must therefore come first so as to be available, I symbolized relations by means of a zero in the right-hand position of the code sequence, whilst terms were represented by unity. Similar arguments gave attributes precedence over entities, passive ideas precedence over active, and the attributive-entitive contrast precedence over that between the static and the changing.

Names and notation for the types

The resulting set of semantic types, with their names and code sequences, was as follows:

> 000 : passive attributive relations (states)
> 001 : passive attributive terms (qualities)
> 010 : passive entitive relations (structures)
> 011 : passive entitive terms (things)
> 100 : active attributive relations (actions)
> 101 : active attributive terms (modes)
> 110 : active entitive relations (activities)
> 111 : active entitive terms (phenomena)

The question arises: Do qualities, actions, phenomena, modes and the other semantic types all behave in a similar way, so that what we know about objects and substances may be applied to them? It seems that they do. The distinction between object and substance has its analogues: phenomena may be divided into events and processes, qualities into positionals and extensives, modes into datals and duratives. Thus an object suffers an event, a substance undergoes a process. Events occur at instants, processes continue over periods. An object may be found at a given place — say the North Pole — while a process extends over a region. As examples, in the realm of phenomena, consider the process we call trade and the event we call making an exchange, the process we call fire and the event we call the oxidation of an atom, the process we call traffic and the event we call the passage of a vehicle, the process we call war and the event we call the firing of a gun. In the realm of qualities, compare orientation with angle, temperature with quantity of heat.

Further, grades corresponding to units, simples, assemblies and the rest are found in respect of all semantic types, not only in respect of things. In the realm of modes, for instance, we are familiar with such measurables as miles per hour and centimetres per second. These are complex ideas made out of simpler notions. They correspond to series: order is important in them. To see this, note that miles per hour is not the same as hours per mile.

Specialists in work study examine trains of events leading to desirable ends and develop methods of reaching the same ends with less effort. Here we encounter typical series of phenomena in the upper biomorphic rank. Another example can be found when a chemical works goes on stream and substances move from vessel to vessel whilst undergoing a sequence of reactions. I should remark that this occurs at molecular level even though the factory in which it takes place is at the level of communities. If substances (for example, sulphuric acid) are subsequently recovered for recycling then the whole cycle of phenomena achieves the status of a system. The Krebs cycle in a living cell is another case of a molecular system within an object of a higher level.

Relations display patterns akin to those of the terms in which they are embodied. The command structure of an army, for example, is a pattern of relations, and so are large numbers of political theories. At the spatial level and below, complex arrangements of relations are found in mathematical formulae, with place-holders to show where the terms (usually numbers) may be inserted. These group the terms into assemblies, series and systems of many sorts. Simple examples are the formula for an arithmetic mean, the pattern made by the elements of a rectangular matrix, and the hypergeometric series.

Full code sequences

The code sequences for semantic types may be added, after

yet another point, to the sequences already given. This adds the triad 011 to the sequences for atoms, nations, and any other objects or substances, so that a full code sequence for Canada is 0.111.1.000.011, or 07103 in octal without the points. If we work entirely within the world of mundane notions, the first zero in this number is superfluous, so that nations may be given the sequence 7103 — seventh level, upper rank, unitary things. Atoms become placed at position 3003, being third level, lower rank unitary things. This way of speaking demands that a zero level be allowed, below the first level, much as a ground floor lies below the first floor of a building. This, of course, is the level of set theory. For example, addition is an assembly action upon the numbers which fit in the lower rank of that level; since numbers are simple attributes, addition is attributive. It gains code sequence 0024 in octal, standing for ground level, lower rank, assembly action. In the longer binary notation this is 000.0.010.100. In both of these sequences a preliminary zero (to indicate mundane ideas) is omitted.

Generics and collectives

While I studied semantic types I found many taxonyms, words naming ideas which group other ideas into classes. I distinguished two varieties of these, the generics and the collectives. To give instances immediately: in respect of a poodle, the notion of a dog is generic and that of a pet is collective. Iodine is generically a halogen but may be collected with other substances as an antiseptic or as a staining agent.

Although generics and collectives of all semantic types appear possible, most of those for which we have names are concerned with objects or substances: that is, with things. Generics are always closely concerned with the construction of the notions they bring together. Iodine is a halogen because of the number of electrons in the outer orbit of each of its atoms. Other elements with the same structure in this respect are also halogens. Iodine is a thing, and so is an electron, and indeed it seems that generic ideas always group ideas of the same semantic type as themselves.

By contrast, a collective idea groups notions which are of a different semantic type from itself. An example is the concept of a weapon. Weapons are things grouped according to a phenomenon, namely their use. Antiques, ironmongery, roofing materials, stock-in-trade, paint, tiles, professors and public relations officers: these, too, are collectives. We live in a world of them.

Generics are easy to place in the pattern of integrative levels. They occupy the position held by the notions they bring together. Collectives, however, tell another story. A rock may be used as a weapon but the concept of a weapon is not fully developed at the molecular level where the rock is found. The proper home for a collective is the lowest grade at which its definition is complete. For example, the notion of a weapon may need an idea from the upper biomorphic rank as one of its constituents. If this is the most advanced idea required, then this is the concept which determines the place which the notion of a weapon must hold.

The holotheme: a provisional summary

It may now be useful to summarize the view I had formed of my subject by the time I had finished this part of my inquiry. Human knowledge, I concluded, is concerned with notions which fall into one or other of two perception classes, the lower of which contains eight clearly defined integrative levels each of two ranks each of eight formative grades each containing eight semantic types each of which may be generic or collective to a greater or less degree. These mundane ideas correspond to daily reality. The remaining notions may do so but await acceptance, or may be known to be fiction, or may of their nature be unprovable. The complete pattern of all ideas may be called the holotheme since other words which might be appropriate are pre-empted for use in representing other meanings by other disciplines. Binary code sequences can be formed in such a way that they act as descriptors of positions in the holotheme, and these may be shortened by transformation to an octal form. The pattern they fix can be found by anyone who makes constructive chains of notions and examines them. Within the class of mundane ideas the pattern is regular, to such a degree that it may even be used to validate notions which seek admittance to it. For example, the four elements of mediaeval cosmology are earth and water, air and fire. These do not fit into the pattern at molecular level as neatly as do atoms, and anyone who tries to use them as subunits, units in the lower rank, of this level will find that the result is an interruption of the major design. It is therefore in order to allot them to the special class, which in the proposed notation follows that of the common or mundane notions.

The holotheme is a pattern of ideas, not of statements; it is no more than a sequential arrangement of the elements of knowledge, based on a design which seems to be inherent in some of these. It has a place for lions, and a place for bravery, and even a place for the bravery of lions, but no place for the statement that lions are brave. Problems about statements, or about how we know what we know, are not its concern.

But it is time to turn to the mathematics.

II

The Development of a Theory

Properties of relations

Students of set theory become familiar with various properties of relations. Since the holotheme seems to be most
neatly arranged if account is taken of how notions are
constructed, and since this is to do with the relations
embodied in the notions, the properties of relations cannot
help but interest those who examine it. The relations dealt
with in set theory hold between subsets of a main set of
terms which is called the full set. The full set is taken to be
one of its own subsets, and the empty set (the set with no
terms in it) is also taken to be a subset of the full set. Every
term in a full set is said to be a member of that full set, and it
is also a member of many of the subsets. Some of the
relations between these subsets of terms are passive, being
conditions; others are active, being operations. Examples of
conditions are overlap, absence, presence, containing,
membership, identicality. Union, intersection and complementation are examples of operations. These relations may
be examined by means of a binary code sequence based on
the properties they possess.

It is convenient to deal with conditions first. Four
properties are relevant, of which the first is reflexiveness. To
place this property first is not an exercise of mere personal
choice: reflexiveness can be defined by the use of one subset
only, and since no relation can be defined by the use of no

subset this makes reflexiveness the first definable property. A condition is reflexive if it relates a subset (or, more generally, any term whatever) to that same subset (or, more generally, that same term). Identicality is reflexive because any subset is identical with itself. Absence is not reflexive because no subset of which we are thinking is at that time absent from our thought. Whatever we may symbolize by the letter A, the absence of A is not A. If in fact the letter A stands for a subset, and if the letter R stands for a relation, we may say that reflexiveness is the condition in which $A\ R\ A$.

The second property is symmetry, which calls for two subsets if it is to be defined. An example is overlap: if A and B are two subsets which have a common member then they are said to overlap each other: A overlaps B and B overlaps A, a condition which we may represent by saying that $A\ R\ B$ and $B\ R\ A$.

The third property is transitivity, which requires three subsets for its definition. The relation of containing is transitive: if A, B and C are three subsets and if A contains B while B contains C then A contains C. We may say that we have a transitive relation when $A\ R\ B$ and $B\ R\ C$ and $A\ R\ C$.

The fourth property differs from the others in that it does not hold between subsets of a full set but between entirely separate full sets — full sets of different varieties, without any common member. So far as I know, this between-set property has no standard name. I have found it convenient to call it 'transversiveness'. The condition of membership is transversive, being between totally different full sets. For example, a man may be a member of the subset of men with blue eyes. Whatever this subset may be, it is certainly not a man. None of the subsets of the full set of men is a man. The full set of subsets has no member in common with the full set of men. Even the subsets consisting of one member only are not themselves men. This effect will be familiar to those who know how an index may be represented by a full set of items (things indexed) crossed by a full set of features (characteristics which, the items may possess). Such a network is called a 'data field', and in it the two full sets — the items and the features — are visibly transverse to each other.

Another example of different varieties of full set may be taken from geometry. Though all triangles are polygons, no triangle is a rectangle. At the degree of specificity at which number of sides matters, triangles and rectangles are members of absolutely different full sets. Relations between these sets are transversive.

Relation codes

These properties of conditions may now be employed as a means of placing the conditions themselves in order. This is done by forming binary code sequences in which the first or right-hand position is used to show the property defined by one term only — reflexiveness. If a condition is reflexive, this position holds the character 1; otherwise 0 is written. The second position deals with the property defined by two terms — symmetry. A symmetric condition is denoted by the character 1; if a condition is not symmetric, 0 is used. The third position is concerned with transitivity, the property defined by means of three terms. Again the possession of the property is shown by 1 and its absence is shown by 0. The fourth, the left-hand, position holds the character 1 if the condition obtains between full sets, and 0 if it is to be found within them — that is, between subsets of a full set.

This is a natural sequence for the properties, being clearly taken from a numeric attribute possessed by the properties themselves — a defining attribute. When the sequence is put to use the results are remarkably neat. To show the method, the condition of containing may be employed. This relation is taken to be not reflexive: it is defined in such a way that things are not permitted to contain themselves. This being so, containing is readily seen to be not transversive, transitive, not symmetric and not reflexive. The pattern of occurrences of the word 'not' in this description is the pattern of zeros in the relation's code sequence: 0100.

The following is a list of conditions found in set theory, from absence (the simplest) to reciprocal membership, which is well into the realm of transversive relations. A point is placed after the symbol which indicates whether the relation concerned is transversive or otherwise. This helps to separate the three well-known properties of reflexiveness, symmetry and transitivity from the less widely treated transversive property, and thus to emphasize whether a condition is found within a full set or between two or more full sets. Here are the conditions:

$$0.000 : absence$$
$$0.001 : presence$$
$$0.010 : disjunction$$
$$0.011 : overlap$$
$$0.100 : containing$$
$$0.101 : inclusion$$
$$0.110 : exclusion$$
$$0.111 : identicality$$
$$1.000 : membership$$
$$1.001 : non-membership$$
$$1.010 : reciprocal membership$$

A few comments on the meanings of the names of these conditions may be helpful. Disjunction is a relation between two subsets which have no common member: it is not transitive because although (in the case of three subsets) the first and second may be disjoint, and the second and third may be disjoint, nevertheless it does not follow that the first and third are disjoint: they may overlap. Inclusion is a form of containing in which a subset is allowed to contain itself. Exclusion, more commonly called mutual exclusion, is a more advanced type of disjunction: here, if there are three subsets, we can be sure that if the first and second are disjoint, and the second and third are disjoint, then the first and third are disjoint also. Membership is a transversive relation between a set of members of subsets and the set of subsets of which they are members. It is an example of a one-way relation between one full set and another. Reciprocal membership is an example of a two-way relationship between full sets. For example, in a data field, the items are members of the features and the features are members of the items.

From the viewpoint of holothemics, this progression of relation code sequences has two properties of outstanding importance. First, it forms a definition series. Every concept it contains can be defined by the use of notions which occur earlier, except for absence, the notion with which it starts. Thus presence is the absence of absence; disjunction is the relation between a present and an absent subset; overlap is the absence of disjunction, containing is the relation between two disjoint subsets and either of them; inclusion holds between a present subset and its overlap with another, exclusion is found amongst many present subsets when these do not overlap; identicality is the absolute absence of exclusion. These brief definitions need expansion and explanation, but they give the flavour of the matter. The principle of definition by means of earlier notions continues into the transversive series.

Secondly, the sixteen code sequences for types of relation correspond exactly with the sixteen sequences representing the ranks and grades of each integrative level. They correspond not only in binary pattern but also in meaning. Thus the examination of notions occurring at higher levels led to the detection of assemblies, mixtures, series and other sorts of idea, which were then observed to exist in the lowest integrative level as well as in the higher levels where they were first detected. These assemblies, mixtures and the like were to do with things; things are held together by their internal relations; and now an examination of relations has produced exactly the same binary pattern, even to the extent of producing a mixture condition (overlap) at the grade where mixtures are found, and a serial condition (containing) where series occur. These conditions of the lowest level seem also to be suited to the higher levels where the pattern was originally found.

As an example of this, consider the condition of being a subsidiary, which occurs between industrial companies. The companies are real: we are concerned with mundane ideas at the communal level. The class and level code is therefore 0.110 (or 06 in octal). The condition applies between companies, not within them, so it is in the upper rank. It is readily seen to be transitive, not symmetric, and not reflexive. Consequently it carries code sequence 1.100 (or 14) for its rank and grade. Finally, being a passive entitive relation, a structure (in this case a structure found in industry) it is of semantic type 010: that is, type 2. Putting all these parts of its code sequence together, the reference 0.110.1.100.010 is achieved, reduced in octal to 06142. This is the holothemic position for the relation, and the way in which the properties of relations are used in order to work it out has been clearly shown.

The relation code sequences throw considerable light on the holothemic pattern. For example, the property of reflexiveness can be seen to correspond to the property of being a substance: the relation code sequences for the grades of simple, mixture, sheet and stretch end with 1, the reflexive symbol. This may seem hard to grasp, but it may help if we recall that substances have been defined as unbounded in at least one direction. In mathematics, there is a well-known connection between the unbounded (the infinite) and the reflexive. An infinite set can be put into one-to-one (reflexive) correspondence with a proper part of itself. Thus there is an infinite set of natural numbers, and there is an infinite set of even natural numbers, and yet the even numbers are only a part of the whole, for odd numbers are part of the whole as well.

It may also help to refer once more to overlap, whose

reflexive grade code sequence, 011, is the sequence for a mixture. This feels right intuitively: what is a mixture but the overlap of two simples, a region in which both of them are found?

The code sequence of overlap incorporates the symmetry symbol, a unit in the middle of the grade triad. Again this is suitable for mixtures: if one substance is mixed with another, that other is mixed with the first. Assemblies also have this sort of symmetry, and their triad — 010, that of disjunction — reminds us that their component parts are disjoint: they do not penetrate each other as the constituents of mixtures do. This is apparent from the zero in the left-hand position, showing the absence of reflexiveness.

The connection between transitivity and the upper four grades in any rank may need less comment. Transitivity is the essence of order, and order is apparent in each of these grades.

Operations

It will now be helpful to consider operations. Operations are active relations and the properties which they possess are not those of reflexiveness, symmetry and transitivity, but of idempotency, commutation and dissociation. Like conditions, operations may be transversive. At the level of set theory this means that they act on whole sets instead of on subsets.

An idempotent operation can be performed on a single term and will leave that term unchanged. If an operation has this property, then its grade triad has a unit in its right-hand position. Otherwise a zero appears there. Using an arrow to stand for 'leads to' or 'results in', the letter R (as before) for a relation, and the letters A, B and C for subsets, we may say that an idempotent operation is one in which $R\ A \longrightarrow A$. Sometimes this is written $A\ R\ A \longrightarrow A$, which is helpful if the operation is normally performed on two subsets. An example is the operation called intersection: this consists in forming the subset consisting of members which two subsets have in common. Some people are children, some are male, and it is possible to possess both features at once, so if we intersect the subset of children with the subset of males there will be a resultant subset, the boys. Intersection of the children with the children produces the children as a resultant subset. The operation is idempotent accordingly. This property can be shown by means of a single term (in this case a subset), and thus coresponds to reflexiveness.

If we possess two subsets on which to operate, then the property of commutation may be shown. A commutative operation is such that the order in which the subsets enter into the operation does not matter. Intersection is commutative as well as idempotent: selecting the males who are children produces the same collection of people as does choosing the children who are males.

If a double-headed arrow is used to signify 'has the same result as' then the commutative property may be symbolized by $A R B \leftrightarrow B R A$.

If an operation can be applied to two subsets, then it can be applied to three if we select a pair out of the three and carry out the operation on these, applying the result, by means of a second instance of the operation, to the remaining subset. Here the order in which the pairs of subsets are taken may affect the final answer. If it does, the operation may be called 'dissociative'. This is not standard terminology. In mathematics, lack of dissociation has been taken as the positive property: it is named 'association' and a dissociative operation is called 'not-associative'. However, if the pattern of occurrences of the word 'not' is to be used as an aid in forming relation code sequences (as it is in the case of conditions) then dissociation must be used as the property which is positive. If a pair of brackets is used, to show which subsets are operated upon first, and if a crossed double-headed arrow is employed to mean 'leads to a different result from', then dissociation may be symbolized by $(A \ R \ B) \ R \ C \leftrightarrow A \ R \ (B \ R \ C)$. The reason for the name of the property may now be clear: the result is affected according to which of its associates is first associated with the central term.

It is easy to check that intersection is not dissociative; so it may be described as not transversive, not dissociative, commutative and idempotent. Thus it has code sequence 0.001 for its rank and grade. If this is compared with the code sequence for the condition of overlap (not transversive, not transitive, symmetric and reflexive — since a subset completely overlaps itself) the two will be found to be the same. In fact, it seems that conditions are closely followed by operations which become possible when the conditions are available. This rule is catered for by the code sequences for semantic types, which place conditions before operations — passive before active. The full octal sequences for overlap and for intersection are 00032 and 00036 respectively.

Although much has been written about the operations of set theory these have not all been provided with standard names. The following list places one or more such operations against the code sequence for each grade of the lower rank of the set-theoretic level, and for this purpose it makes use of one or two names which are not in common use.

> 0.000 : complementation
> 0.001 : conservation
> 0.010 : adjunction
> 0.011 : union, intersection
> 0.100 : relative complementation
> 0.101 : restriction
> 0.110 : nand, nor
> 0.111 : counter nand, counter nor

Of these, complementation, intersection and union are dealt with in all works on set theory. Intersection (choosing the members common to both of two subsets) has been mentioned above. Union consists in choosing the members of one, the other, or both of two subsets. Complementation consists in choosing the members of a full set which are not members of the subset which is complemented. Conservation is the stay-the-same operation, and as such it is generally ignored. Works which treat set theory in some depth are likely to mention relative complementation — choosing the members of one given subset which are not members of another. If only one subset is available, it is rejected. Adjunction is less likely to appear: it is the formation of the subset consisting of members of two named subsets which do not have common members: it appears, that is to say, before overlap is available. Restriction is not a standard name: here it refers to the operation choosing a named subset but omitting from it any members which are also members of another named subset. If only one subset is available, it is chosen.

The nand and nor operations are widely used in the logic of electronic circuits. The first, the 'not-and' operation, consists in forming the subset of all members of a full set which are not members of both of two named subsets. Thus it is the complement of intersection. It is sometimes known as rejection, or as the Scheffer operation, after the theoretician who paid special attention to it. In the same way, the nor operation, not-or, is the complement of union. The counter operations to these, at the highest grade in the rank, are formed by means of an operation of complementation acting on nand or on nor. This has the effect of making nand and nor idempotent (for example, not neither A nor A is obviously A). The names 'counter nand' and 'counter nor' are not standard.

Numbers

Sets and subsets are basic entities. Their qualities are numbers, which are basic attributes. Specifically, the qualities appropriate to present subsets are positive natural numbers. Zero is appropriate to the empty subset. Negative natural numbers, so to speak, suit absent subsets. The negative and positive natural numbers, with zero, form the integers. When a full set has been attained it becomes possible to relate subsets to it; these relations are accompanied by relations between the natural numbers or the integers exhibited by the subset and the full set. Thus a new type of number, the rational number, appears. Rational numbers occur in the upper rank of the set-theoretic level, where they take part in a pattern which is similar to that of the natural numbers in the lower rank. Rationals whose value is less than unity correspond to negative naturals, and those whose value is greater than unity correspond to those of the positive sort. Unity itself, the so-called identify element of multiplication, corresponds to zero, the identity element of addition; and as might be expected these two operations occur in their appropriate ranks – multiplication in the upper, being an operation between the numbers appropriate to full sets, and addition in the lower, being an operation between disjoint subsets.

The following is a selection of numeric conditions and operations found in the set-theoretic level, together with their rank and grade code sequences:

0.000 : being negative	succession; inversion about zero
0.001 : being positive	
0.010 :	addition
0.011 :	cyclic addition
0.100 : being greater than	subtraction
0.101 : being greater than or equal to	cyclic subtraction
0.110 :	subtraction of a sum $(-(p+q))$
0.111 : equality	
1.000 : being fractional	inversion about unity
1.001 : being whole	
1.010 : being relatively prime	multiplication
1.011 : having common factors	forming the highest common factor
1.100 : being properly divisible	division
1.101 :	
1.110 :	division by a multiple $(1/pq)$
1.111 : congruence	averaging

This pattern is rich in relationships. A simple example is afforded by the operations whose code sequences end in zero. These may be compared, rank against rank, as follows:

(grade)	(lower rank)	(upper rank)
000	: inversion about zero	inversion about unity
010	: addition	multiplication
100	: subtraction	division
110	: subtraction of a sum	division by a multiple

Another example is obtained by comparing both entitive and attributive relations, taking these from just one rank and grade, as follows:

rank 0, grade 100, semantic type
- 000 : being greater than
- 010 : containing
- 100 : subtraction
- 110 : relative complementation

Here the great similarity between relations of the same rank and grade is obvious. If one subset contains another, its natural number (the number of its members) is greater than that of the other. If we form a relative complement, consisting of members of the larger subset which are not members of the smaller, then at the same time we subtract the natural number of the smaller subset from that of the larger.

Mathematical structures

When I have a problem it pushes itself into my thoughts in all the spare moments of the day. During meals I produce numberless jottings on the backs of envelopes, and I end train journeys with diagrams and statements and questions and bits of explanatory paragraphs on sheets of paper pushed hastily into my briefcase as my destination arrives. Such was my exploration of the relation code sequences of the set-theoretic level. I was fascinated by the interlinked patterns I found there. Each new discovery added to my feeling that this was the genuine one and only foundation for the arrangement of notions in the higher levels of the holotheme. The most powerful reinforcement of this view, however, was my sudden realization that the relation code sequence embodied a complete series of mathematical structures in exact and proper order. This series, in order of increasing complexity, is: semigroup, group, ring, field, vector space. Briefly, a semigroup is an arrangement in which addition is possible; a group permits both addition and subtraction; in a ring addition, subtraction and multiplication can be carried out; in a field, addition, subtraction, multiplication and division are all available; in a vector space, more advanced operations can be employed: an example is involution.

If the rank and grade code sequences for the operations upon numbers are examined in succession, it becomes clear that the first four provide all that is necessary for two semigroups — one of the positive natural numbers, and one of the negative natural numbers, acted on by addition. The next four add what is needed for a group, bringing the semigroups together to form the set of integers, in which subtraction is always possible. It may be noted that an integer is often defined as a set of ordered pairs of natural numbers, any one of which pairs may represent it; and the introduction of order is typical of the transitive and dissociative upper parts of an integrative rank.

These eight grades of the lower rank, containing the ingredients of what is called a group under addition, are followed by a further eight which, in the higher rank, hold the material for a group under multiplication. The first four of these upper eight contain two semigroups as before, one dealing with fractions and the other with whole numbers: this time the semigroup operation is multiplication, and division is introduced in the second four to form the complete group. Again a new type of number is created: fractions and whole numbers form rational numbers, and these are often defined as ordered pairs of simpler numbers, any one of which pairs may represent its appropriate rational.

The additive group with the two higher semigroups form a ring; when the entire level is taken all together, its two ranks, each with its group, form a field. Very neatly indeed, the set-theoretic level is a mathematical field, pure and simple. It is to be inferred that every subsequent level is, in its mathematics, a field also.

This leaves vector spaces unaccounted for. A vector space is a collection of elements which form a group for a commutative operation, and which are subject to all the operations of a field: for example, there is a vector space of polynomials. To exhibit an instance: the polynomial $5x^4 + 3x^3 + 9x^2$ can be multiplied (this is the field operation) by the rational number 6½. The commutative operation of the group of terms of the polynomial is the sort of addition symbolized by the plus sign in the example; the field operation happens ·in this case to be multiplication, but it could as easily have been addition, division or subtraction.

The terms of polynomials are the units of the next integrative level, the level of spaces. In this level, polynomials play the part of integers. The lower rank is the rank of the real numbers, which have polynomial representations – for example, a decimal representation. Their vector space lies in one dimension just as, one level below, the proto-space of subsets of a full set may be represented as one dimension in a data field. In the upper rank, vector spaces of many dimensions appear, and in this rank the typical number is complex. Complex numbers may be represented by vectors in a vector space of two dimensions, and also as two-part numbers consisting of a real number linked to an imaginary number (which is a real number multiplied by $\sqrt{-1}$). They may also be shown as a particular type of rational fraction, a fraction whose numerator and denominator are polynomials. Here they show their character as space-level brothers of rational numbers, which at set-theoretic level may be shown as ratios of integers, and which (like complex numbers) occupy an upper rank.

FIGURE 4: Some of the structures found in mathematics, related to some of the notions encountered in the set-theoretic level

	mathematical structure	binary grade number	notions encountered in the grade
	SEMIGROUP	0.000	succession; inversion about zero; negativity
		0.001	being positive
		0.010	addition
		0.011	cyclic addition
	GROUP	0.100	subtraction; being greater than
		0.101	being greater than or equal to
		0.110	the operation '-(p+q)'
		0.111	equality
	RING	1.000	inversion about unity; being fractional
		1.001	being whole
		1.010	multiplication; being relatively prime
		1.011	forming the highest common factor
	FIELD	1.100	division; being properly divisible
		1.101	being divisible
		1.110	the operation '1/pq'
		1.111	averaging (arithmatic mean); congruence
VECTOR SPACE in next integrative level			

All the notions given above are to do with numbers and only a few of those available are given. Cyclic addition is idempotent because $p + p$ (mod p) is p: it has affinities with the set-theoretic operations of union and intersection. The numeric counterpart of the intersection of two different overlapping subsets is addition modulo p where p is the number of members in the union of the two.

'Proper' divisibility excludes the operation of dividing a number by itself.

Complex numbers may also be represented as a special sort of matrix, and matrices are sets of interlinked vectors. For example, a square matrix of order two is a set of four numbers, displayed as two rows of two numbers each. Each row is a vector; each column is a vector. It is remarkably similar in its looks to a data field relating one full set to another. Matrices are found in the upper rank of the spatial level, and may be used to represent the displacements, rotations, reflections, shears and other transformations of geometric shapes. The entities of the spatial level are indeed shapes of this type, and of course their component parts, down to the simplest part, a point. The algebraic representation of geometry, which gave so powerful an impetus to the development of mathematics when it was recognized, arises because at the spatial level geometric figures are accompanied by appropriate numbers just as sets are accompanied by numbers at the set-theoretic level.

It may be of interest here to display the level, rank and grade code sequences of a few notions in the spatial level. This level contains many more ideas than does the level below it, and in consequence the following are the merest handful compared with the number which are available for study.

001.0.001 : being a power of. Powers are powers of rational (or higher) numbers; the reflexiveness arises because any such number is a power — the first — of itself. Multiplied by suitable coefficients, using the contents of the set-theoretic level for this purpose, the powers become the terms of polynomials, and indeed may be thought of as the simplest form of polynomial in their own right.

001.0.100 : extracting the root. Many roots are irrational: here is the heart of the matter so far as a large class of real numbers is concerned. The grade triad is identical with that of division one rank below and with that of subtraction two ranks below. Just as root extraction (involution) has its connections with real numbers, so division is connected with rationals and subtraction with integers. The relation code sequences reflect this.

001.0.111 : forming a geometric mean ($\sqrt{xy}$). Compare the grade triad with that for averaging (forming an arithmetic mean). In each case the operation consists of assembling a number of terms by means of an operation of grade 010 and then applying the result to an operation of grade 100 which is attached to a number which is the number of terms entering into the first operation.

001.1.000 : being imaginary (of a number); forming an inner product of vectors; matrix conformation (that is, matrix multiplication).

001.1.010 : the operation $\sqrt{x^2 + y^2}$. This gives the length of a vector in terms of its components along two axes at right angles to each other. It also gives the argument of a complex number expressed in polar co-ordinates. In the form $r = \sqrt{x^2 + y^2}$ it is the equation of a circle. In passing, the condition of being-at-right-angles also has code sequence 001.1.010.

This may be sufficient to show how the code sequences continue into and through the higher level of the domain of mathematics. Before leaving this (with an apology for concentrating so much upon numbers) it may be of interest to return to the very beginning and to look at the so-called Peano axioms for the formation of the natural numbers on which all higher mathematics is built. These axioms begin with the existence of zero, and zero has code sequence 0.000.0.000.001 (mundane, ground level, lower rank, lowest grade, quality). In passing, zero embodies the condition of nullity – 0.000.0.000.000. The axioms proceed by using the operation of succession, which (like zero) is at grade 000. Its full code sequence is 0.000.0.000.100. The result is to produce the number one, unity, as the successor of zero. This process is then repeated to produce the later natural numbers. It is satisfactory to note that this well-known means of obtaining the natural numbers begins where it should, at the beginning.

Into the domain of physics

Sub-atomic physics gains powerful support from mathematics. It is interesting to see how the relation code pattern may continue from the higher rank of the spatial level into the lower sub-atomic rank. For this purpose the basic measurables which loom so large in physics and chemistry may be examined: mass, length, time and energy. Length appears in the lower spatial rank, with the arrival of the real numbers and of continuity. Time occurs in the upper rank of the same level, where the spacetime continuum is developed. If the lower subatomic rank begins with photons and other particles without rest-mass, then this is where energy appears. Mass then follows, coming into its own in the higher rank of the subatomic level where it is manifest in the electron, the muon, the proton, the neutron and other massy particles.

Given length, time and energy, a definition of mass is possible: mass is calculated by first multiplying energy by time-squared, and then dividing the result by length-squared. Of course, these are not ordinary multiplications and divisions: we are in the presence of new operations, which are not too unlike the ordinary multiplication and division of integers or rational numbers. It is not common practice to define mass in terms of energy, length and time: the usual process is to define energy, which is done by means of length, time and mass. In the present case, however, this is not possible: mass comes last: if we seek a definition sequence based on a relation code then the notions to hand are the earlier ones.

Mass is not the only physical measurable which can be defined by the use of two or more of the trio, energy, time and length. Many others can be so defined: spin, action, power, force, surface tension, gravity and the like. Since these are based on properties suited to substances rather than to objects — for example, the time is a duration, the length is a distance rather than a position — their grade triads end in unity. The following is a selection of these measurables, each with its level, rank and grade, and with an indication of order of precedence within grades:

010.0.011 : $E\,T$: angular momentum, spin, action
               $E\,T^2$: moment of inertia

010.0.101 : $E\,/\,L$: force
               $E\,/\,L^2$: surface tension
               $E\,/\,L^3$: stress, gravity
               $E\,/\,T$: power

010.0.111 : $E\,T/L$: momentum
               $E\,T^2/L^2$: mass

Here, of course, E stands for energy, L stands for length and T refers to time. The similarity between the formula for mass and those for an arithmetic and a geometric mean is worth noting. Again we have a commutative but not dissociative operation combined with a dissociative operation which is not commutative to produce an operation which is both commutative and dissociative. It is also noteworthy how near mass is to the next rank, the rank in which it is embodied in massy particles. When I first encountered this part of the pattern, I was impressed also by the obvious interpretation of gravity as three-dimensional surface tension, a sort of effect of space stretching out, trying to be spacious, and thus bringing bodies together much as I have seen two needles, gently floating on the surface of very still water, come together by two-dimensional surface tension effects.

Relation codes and the holotheme

As I explored the pattern of relation code sequences in the domain of mathematics, it seemed that I was doing three things at once, or perhaps one thing in three disguises. I was trying to work out a mathematical model to provide an underlying theory for my arrangement of everyday notions taken from higher positions in the holotheme. I was placing ideas in the first two integrative levels just as I would place them in higher levels, using the same rules and the same collection of semantic types, formative grades, higher and lower ranks. I was discovering a classification for the

discipline of mathematics itself. The theory or model I
sought, and the actual arrangement of ideas to be found in
the lowest levels of all, were one and the same thing. I
remember looking at the symbols for relations between
terms, scouring the pages of textbooks of all degrees of
difficulty, and finding none that were not one or other of my
four semantic types of relation. Nor did I find any
mathematical term which was not a passive or active entity or
a passive or active attribute. As I followed the series of
relation codes upwards through the level of space and into
the subatomic level where energy and matter appeared, I
began to feel I was doing no more than unroll, with great
labour, a chart of an ocean which was already well-known to
everyone but myself.

At the same time I knew that other workers at the trade of
organising knowledge had reached opinions at variance with
mine. Most of these provided a pattern which was far less
regular than my set of relation code sequences, a pattern
whose very complexity seemed more in keeping with the
bewildering ramifications of knowledge than did my rigid
binary scheme. Certainly a binary framework is suspiciously
neat. I can understand the view that, perhaps unwittingly, I
started with it and forced a large number of notions into the
pigeonholes it provides. However, I do not think this was so.
I knew nothing of set theory when I began, and the notation
I used in order to handle entities and attributes in the early
days of my inquiry was based on the alphabet. The pattern of
noughts and ones came later, and this helped to persuade me
of its validity.

What impressed me most, however, was the sense of
surprise I so often felt as bits of the pattern fell into place.
Such unexpected pleasures came, for example, when I
realized that the relation code sequences put mathematical
structures in order from semigroup to vector space, when I
found that they put relations into a definition series and
when I saw how they could be equated with the binary code

sequences I had derived as a result of looking at ideas taken from levels much higher than that of set theory and arithmetic.

Another impressive aspect of the pattern was that it seemed to have predictive properties. To choose an instance from the cytomechanic level: I knew nothing about cellular biology, but the repeating pattern of units and subunits implied that I ought to find, inside the living cell, something made out of molecules by the stages of assembling, forming series, and assembling series into systems. I looked at articles on the subject and found much about polyribosomes, nucleoli and the endoplasmic reticulum. I also found the mitochondrion, an organelle complete with its own enclosing membrane assembled out of standard protein and phospholipid molecules. The mitochondrion contained assemblies which formed series of specialized parts, and these transferred electrons from place to place in the course of building up molecules which acted as energy stores. These operations were reversible: there was a means of releasing energy as well as of capturing it. I was in the presence of the typical balancing effect of a system. I wrote the phospholipids and the mitochondrion into one of my chains of notions, as I have already shown.

Rules for placing notions

Thus I decided the relation code pattern was that of the holotheme itself. I might, I knew, be mistaken; but as my inquiry continued I came more and more to feel that the mistakes were likely to be in the detail rather than in the broad outline of the arrangement. It was, I concluded, time to develop rules for placing ideas according to the code. This was not difficult: it was merely a formalization of the way I habitually found what I thought was the right code sequence for a notion I sought to place. However, though it was easy, it was important. It was a step towards finding how hard it might be to teach the method to others.

Here is a typical series of placement rules:

> First, write down your definition of the meaning of the word you wish to place.
>
> Next, consider the notion to which it refers or any representation of the notions it groups together.
>
> In respect of this, ask:
> ... Is it generally accepted as mundane, irrespective of faith, school or persuasion (0) or is it a matter of belief, fiction or hypothesis (1)?
>
> From your answer, write down the code numeral for the significance class.
>
> Next, ask:
> ... What is the highest unit which it contains or to which it refers or of which it is a representative? In which integrative level is this unit?
> ... Is this unit in the lower (0) or the upper (1) rank of the level?
>
> From your answers, write down the code sequence for the integrative level and rank.
>
> Next, ask:
> ... Is it, or does it embody, a relation which is: intransitive or associative (0) or otherwise (1)? non-symmetric or non-commutative (0) or otherwise (1)? not reflexive or not idempotent (0) or otherwise (1)?
>
> From your answers, write down the code sequence for the formative grade.
>
> Next, ask:
> ... Is it passive (0) or active (1)?
> ... Is it attributive (0) or entitive (1)?

. . . Is it a relation (0) or a term (1)?

From your answers, write down the code sequence for the semantic type.

These answers in this order will produce a code sequence for class, level, grade and type. Convert it to any shorter notation which may be in use, if this is necessary.

Last, ask:
. . . Is this sufficient, or is further specificity needed?

If the answer is 'yes', apply these placement rules again or use such other rules as may have been chosen so as to achieve the additional specificity required.

This is a long series of choices, but experience in making them soon leads to speed. The class, level and rank are often seen at a glance; the formative stage and the semantic type are supplied in the definition if it is based constructively on suitable units. The rules are only called upon in difficult cases, and many of these arise only because the definition is poor. Improvements in this lead to immediate placement of the notion concerned.

The pattern in brief

Again it is time to summarize. The pattern of notions derived from a study of ideas arranged in constructive order includes, quite naturally, a portion which applies to the simplest, the most fundamental and in a sense the most abstract notions. These are the concepts used in arithmetic and set theory. It transpires that this part of the pattern can be derived by means of a very easy rule from the properties of the relations between terms — natural numbers and subsets — and that the result is a very vast neat arrangement of the notions in use at the set-theoretic level, the ground level of the holotheme.

This caters for all semantic types at each grade in each rank of the level, and can be extended directly to cater for the next level, the level of spaces. Consequently it covers the whole of mathematics, and places the group, ring, field and vector space framework of the subject in the order it is already known to possess. It continues from thence into the

FIGURE 5: The nesting property in the structure of binary relation code sequences, which corresponds to the many nesting and repetitive patterns in the holetheme. The stops or points which break up the code sequences as shown in the text are here omitted

0	0	0	0	0	0
0	0	0	0	0	1
0	0	0	0	1	0
0	0	0	0	1	1
0	0	0	1	0	0
0	0	0	1	0	1
0	0	0	1	1	0
0	0	0	1	1	1
0	0	1	0	0	0
0	0	1	0	0	1
0	0	1	0	1	0
0	0	1	0	1	1
0	0	1	1	0	0
0	0	1	1	0	1
0	0	1	1	1	0
0	0	1	1	1	1
0	1	0	0	0	0
0	1	0	0	0	1
0	1	0	0	1·	0
0	1	0	0	1	1
0	1	0	1	0	0

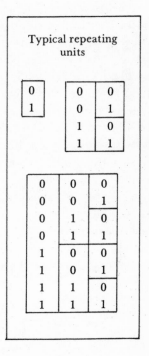

Typical repeating units

subatomic level without difficulty, where it handles the placing of such physical measurables as action, momentum, gravity and mass.

The nested structure of groups, rings, fields and spaces is reflected in a nested structure of the binary code sequences which provide positions for the notions of the mathematical domain. This nesting continues upwards through all the integrative levels and indicates that the pattern continues in actuality. It reflects the fact that mathematics can be applied to any higher notion: mathematics is embedded at the core of the larger scheme.

Thus the set theoretic level provides a model or a theory for the remainder of the holothemic system. This can be used to develop a series of rules for placing ideas at any grade of any level, whether mundane or special. The rules consist of a series of choices, and can be displayed as an algorithm or logical tree structure. The series is fairly long, as befits the complexity of knowledge; but many groups of choices can be made simultaneously, which makes the operation swift. The resulting positions, to which the notions under consideration are allotted, can be validated by reference to the rule that each notion should be definable in accordance with its construction, by reference to earlier notions. If this proves possible, the place it occupies is acceptable and should normally be the lowest place it can occupy while still meeting the definition requirement. Thus a notion's position is the least upper bound of its definition sequence.

Thus the constructive order of ideas is provided with a mathematical basis and a series of rules for its application.

III

Background and Comment

Some other views

As the binary theory of the holotheme became increasingly persuasive, as the various parts of it came together, I began to discuss it with friends and colleagues as well as to compare it with other accounts of the matter in the existing literature. I soon realized it was nothing like self-evident. To start with, it was suspect on the ground that it was too neat. The mathematics were regarded with incomprehension, suspicion and at times dislike. Though many — perhaps most — arrangements of the sciences have begun with mathematical notions, the body of opinion which could not easily accept a fundamental position for the science of sets and numbers remained large. I concluded that much effort in the field of general classification was nullified by unrecognized pre-conceived opinions, lack of certain types of knowledge, and concentration upon words instead of upon the notions these represent. There was general agreement that something like integrative levels existed; the problems arose when attempts were made to identify them.

As I studied the history I was impressed by the extent to which the major sciences had had to develop before it had become possible to display anything like a complete sequence of degrees of complexity in the world around us. In the past, the domains of mathematics and of the physical sciences had been separated by unknown land, while another wide stretch of ignorance had lain between the physical sciences and biology. Mathematical set and number theory was not available as a unifying subject, and anyone who detected a pattern in part of the holotheme could follow it but a very little way. The criticism which can be made of work done after these gaps were closed is quite unfair if levied on earlier schemes for organizing knowledge. As I read, it seemed to me there was a great divide between the late nineteenth and the mid twentieth century. Before this divide, praise was due for the avoidance of pitfalls, but it was hard to blame those who fell into them. After it, different rules applied. The frontiers of the great domains of knowledge had been pushed back till they met; the countryside was mapped, at least in outline. Pitfalls were visible: no praise was now due for avoiding them. On the other hand, it was fair to regard falling into one as calling for a little censure.

There are now several widely-held views which, in the light of this development of the sciences, seem to me to be mistaken. There is, for example, a wish to base an integrative level on the mind and its creations. This is a continuance of a tendency which has been with us for many centuries. It takes several forms. The notions of mathematics may be given a home above the level of whole plants and animals, on the ground that a mind is needed in order that they may be formed or comprehended. A psychological level may be said to exist, above that of biology and below that of society, with mind as its prime inhabitant. These views may occur together. Attempts may be made to form an integrative level out of mentefacts: creations of the mind, much as artefacts are (but are they?) creations of the hand. These views may be called instances of a psychocentric fallacy. So far as the relation code sequences are concerned, adoption of this opinion leads to a break in the continuity of the structural pattern. The pattern demands that more complicated entities in this advanced domain should be made out of simpler ones; but the mind is not constructed out of human beings, or definable only by using the notion of a complete animal of any sort. It is, I suppose, possible that a break of this type really occurs; but I have not been able to bring myself to believe so. It seems far simpler to treat the mind as a phenomenon, the brain in action, amazingly skilful, flexible and creative, yet easily sent awry, as are the other functions of the body. Speaking for myself, my feelings, memories, sensations, emotions, habits, impulses seem to be inside me, and I find it straightforward to call my mind a phenomenon of the lower biomorphic level in consequence.

Another example of this kind of mistake is the thinking which provides different levels for plants, the lower animals, and mankind. This has a long history. From early times a mineral level has also been used, placed under that of the vegetables. The whole series then runs from mineral, vegetable and animal to abstract — the abstract providing the mental element which is taken as typical of human beings. Like many other arrangements which do not tally with the relation codes, this is none the less a powerful means of locating notions. Clearly no criticism can be levelled against it from a holothemic viewpoint if its object is not to model reality as well as may be, but simply to offer an effective classifying device.

Other fallacies are of the dimensional type. Of these, a good example is the belief that to be later in time is to be more advanced in complexity. This is true as a general trend over long periods of time: the occupants of the biomorphic level have certainly appeared on earth much later than those of the molecular, and a theory of continuous creation is needed if we are to argue that all levels are found here or there in the universe at the same time, whatever that may mean. So far, so good; but there are forces at work which reduce the higher to the lower, and these have led to the postulation of the existence of disintegrative levels which hold the broken bits of higher things. Setting aside the question of what may be meant by a broken bit of a mode or a quality, the attempt to set up disintegrative levels makes it impossible to place — for example — an oxygen atom. Is it disintegrated water, or integrated subatomic particles? The better course is not to trouble about origins, but only about internal structure. Origins, from this viewpoint, are irrelevant.

The dimensions of space also contribute to confusion. There is a tendency to feel that larger aggregates occupy higher levels than do smaller amounts. This leads to a suggestion that aggregative, as opposed to integrative, levels exist. The problem here is that there is nowhere to stop. It is simpler to return to set theory and to recall that a larger set is simply a larger set, and that is all.

Laws of the levels

Much work on integrative levels has been carried out by J.K. Feibleman. In *Focus on Information and Communication* (*ASLIB*, London, 1965) he lists the following major levels: the physical; the chemical; the biological; the psychological; the anthropological. He mentions a level of geometry below physics, and his anthropological level includes human institutions and cultures, thus extending the pattern up to the higher rank of the national level. He comments: 'The picture seems unfinished because of the dead ends and also because of the asymmetry of the whole.' As I write, Feibleman's account is already seven years old, but this does not take it back beyond the point at which all the evidence for a more consistent pattern was available. If my argument is correct, then Feibleman's work leaves out large parts of the domains of mathematics and of the social sciences, while inserting a mental level in the best traditions of the psychocentric fallacy. Removing the intrusive level, and applying relation code techniques to the remainder, we go far to produce the more coherent arrangement which he sought. It is fair to add that his article ends with the question, 'Are there infra-geometrical and supra-cultural levels which have thus far escaped our sensibilities and our instruments?' As to the infra-geometrical, it is clear I would answer 'Yes'. The supra-cultural is a different matter. If the cultural level may be equated with the national, then anything supra-cultural will, in the language of these pages, be in the higher perception class. Perhaps that is right; but again, perhaps it is just a matter of how we define the meanings of our words.

In the same work, which is a revision of an earlier article in the British Journal for the Philosophy of Science (May, 1954), Feibleman presents a considerable number of laws relating the levels to each other. The following are examples:

> ... the higher the level, the greater the complexity of entities.
> ... in any entity, the higher level depends upon the lower.
> ... the later the date, the higher the level of organization.
> ... in any entity the lower level is directed by the higher.

The concept of laws of the levels is very attractive, but for my part I should like to see laws of a more specific type than these. For example, is it true to say that qualities of higher levels arise from the phenomena found below them? Colour is a case in point: it may be a quality at molecular level, but it stems from the wavelength of light, and vibration of photons is a phenomenon of the subatomic variety. Does length at the spatial level arise from a change in numeric measure at the set-theoretic? Is the honesty of a community a result of the frequency with which its individual members perform honest actions? This looks like a reasonable law, which may give insight into the construction of ideas at many levels. But are there other sources of qualities? And what about modes? Modes are the qualities of phenomena, which are things in course of alteration; if qualities arise from lower phenomena, do modes arise from lower things? Acidity may be a mode at molecular level, but it is measured by finding the concentration of hydrogen ions in the solution in question, and hydrogen ions are protons, so that the measure arises in the subatomic level, and is to do with things, as suggested.

If laws of this type can be found, they will give the student of the holotheme something to get his or her teeth into.

The arrival of new levels

This may be a suitable point at which to discuss a few problems, chosen more or less at random, concerned with the way the higher grades and levels develop from the lower. These are further examples of the matter from which reliable laws of the levels may one day be derived.

The first of these problems concerns the case of the feather and the bird. The question is: How does the holotheme unroll in such a way that feathers need not be developed before birds appear, even though feathers are constructive parts of birds? It is of course possible to argue flatly that the question arises from the temporal version of the dimensional fallacy, and therefore should not be asked. It deserves more respect, however.

We are familiar with one-member sets in mathematics, and with one-man companies, single-cell animals, and one-city nations like Monaco and Singapore. The atoms of inert gases can be thought of as single-atom molecules in view of their lack of valency. In all these cases the same entity seems to be an inhabitant of two levels at once, depending on how it is regarded. If we look at set-theory we can see in a general way what occurs.

We start with the one-member sets. Full sets of this type can show no internal structure even though, as full sets, they occupy the start of the upper rank of their level. However, at this position there must be at least some inhabitants with internal structure, since otherwise the lower rank would be unstructured. Fortunately we do not have far to look. Sets with as few as two members display structure: in this case the structure of an assembly.

Such a two-member framework is simple, however. To show how simple, we need only consider the condition of overlap — rank and grade code 0.011. A two-member full set cannot show this, since it cannot be divided into subsets which have a common member and a different member. Only a full set of three or more members can provide this facility. In short, if we have to build a set of at least three members before much internal structure can be displayed, it is clear that higher units may at times hold too few lower units to reveal all the intervening degrees of complexity. This is what transpires to be the case in practice in higher ranks and levels.

This is why birds and their feathers may arrive simultaneously: the birds bring their feathers with them, just as a sufficiently large set brings alll its subsets with it.

Aggregates of matter

The series unit — simple — assembly — mixture — series — sheet — system — stretch has already been described. It is the series of grades on the passive entitive side of the holotheme. It suggests that the most inclusive course through the available notions of things may run alternately from the bounded to the boundless and then back to the bounded, and then to the boundless again, and so on. An example is the progression from a carbon atom, a unit, through the simple carbon to an assembly, a diamond.

At the upper rank of the molecular level this progression may be examined at grade 101, where boundless expanses of molecular materials may be found. Sheets of this type need not be infinite even though they are boundless: for example, like the air or the sea or the upper mantle of the earth they may curve round to form the atmosphere, the hydrosphere and the lithosphere; and it will be noted that outer shells include inner shells. The relation of inclusion, we note from set theory, carries the same grade code as that of a sheet — namely, 101. This is intriguing. The earth is a finite but unbounded laminate of sheets of the upper molecular rank. This remark disregards our planet's coat of life, but is quite satisfactory from the viewpoint of astrophysics.

Two further grades are available in the holotheme after this, before the domain of the physical sciences is complete. The solar system may perhaps be an inhabitant of one of these. It is not merely larger than the earth: it is more complex. It is a system in the meaning here adopted for the word: the sun and its planets are held together by counterbalancing forces. If solar systems are in the penultimate grade of the molecular level, as this may indicate, what occupies the highest grade, before the cytomechanic level begins? It may be that the physical universe as a whole is to be placed in this position. It certainly seems to be unbounded, which is in keeping with the grade code sequence 111.

All this is highly speculative, but shows how the relation code can be used in the business of placing elements of the cosmos in order. This approach may be contrasted with other attacks on the problem: for example, the suggestion that aggregative levels exist, to cater for collections of gross material bodies. This has already been mentioned, as an instance of a dimensional fallacy.

Photons

The lowest rank of the domain of physical science, like the highest, is currently the site of intense and costly effort, both intellectually and by way of a great investment in equipment. Somewhere between the photon and the electron there lie — if the relation code is right — assemblies, series and systems of objects which are yet to be found, or at any rate identified among what is already known. 'Here be quarks' is written somewhere on the map of this misty territory. It is interesting that sine waves appear to possess the highest relation code sequence in the spatial level, and that the photons which immediately follow them are described by means of two such waves, an electric and a magnetic component, at right angles to each other along a common axis, and out of phase in such a way that the locus of the point of intersection is a helix. Of course, to visualize a point of intersection in this way it is helpful to think of the waves as corrugated planes. The vision of these little intersection points screwing themselves along at incredible speed, perhaps aided by a displacement of one set of waves along the axis in relation to the other set, is one of the means I have tried to use in imagining the quanta of quantum theory. If only they would roll themselves up into closed circuits they might act like tiny gyroscopes and produce effects of inertia leading to mass. Such imagining is dangerous: one gets laughed at by the experts. Perhaps it may be best to keep quiet, after noting that if quarks exist and are found – as predicted – to build up into subatomic particles with rest mass, they may well turn out to be what the relation code knows as systems. Systems are usually hard to separate from the unit in which they are embodied. Perhaps that is why quarks are so elusive.

However these problems may be resolved, these notes about the quark and the cosmos, the feather and the bird, may serve to indicate how the relation code sequence may generate a speculative attitude, out of the very attempt to place ideas in accordance with it. These are the sorts of exercise which are likely to yield specific laws of construction connecting levels, ranks, grades, and semantic types in a consistent way.

Other recent work

As I write, the most recent work which is to hand on these

topics is the Library Association's Research Pamphlet Number One: 'Classification and Information Control' (London, 1969). This contains a series of papers representing the work of the Classification Research Group from 1960 to the year of publication. Since these display the stages of an inquiry which is still in progress, they are not always consistent with each other, and show several alternative views of their subject. They are a most convenient source of examples for any study of the problems encountered during the search for integrative levels and for a classification of notions based upon them. The principal paper is Derek Austin's 'The Theory of Integrative Levels Reconsidered as a Basis for a General Classification'. If my present views are accepted, then several of the engaging sidetracks have been taken here, including that which leads to the dimensional fallacy, with its requirement for aggregative levels, and that which leads to a viewpoint from which the problem of the bird and its feathers appears forbidding.

Oliver L. Reiser's *The Integration of Human Knowledge* (Boston, 1958) presents a philosopher's approach to the study of integrative levels. It offers no specifically patterned approach, such as can be obtained by way of relation code sequences, but presents much relevant material (for example, in the region between mathematics and the upper level of the physical domain) and comments on many of the effects arising from the existence of the levels. Reiser remarks, for example, on the curious property of the square root of minus one, which is a component of complex numbers in one of their forms, noting that it sends matters 'off at right angles' to their previous direction. This he takes to be a typical sign of the arrival of a new stage of integration, and his opinion seems to be confirmed by the way the condition of being off at right angles is found again and again in the relation code pattern. It first appears in a primitive form when two full sets are related to each other in the upper rank of the set theoretic level by means of a data field diagram of rows intersected by columns. It also resides in the upper rank of the spatial level, where complex numbers appear in essentially the way Reiser mentions. It is encountered in the relations between the semantic types, which can be shown by means of a cube diagram whose relation-term axis is at right angles to the entity-attribute axis while both are orthogonal to the passive-active axis. On the active side the systems of differential equations used by Bertalanffy in 'An Outline of General System Theory' (*British Journal for the Philosophy of Science*, 1950, vol. 1) display the same effect. These are used for representing the behaviour of biological systems, and show the typical rectangular pattern of rows and columns. Bertalanffy's aim is not to explore the pattern of integrative levels, however: it is to set up a general theory of the interacting elements of systems wherever they may occur. In essence, this is to study the whole of the active side of the holotheme, dealing in the end with every notion whose relation code has a unit in the first position of the final binary triad, signifying an active semantic type. Using the symbol x as a place-holder, this means all notions with a binary level, rank, grade and type code sequence of the form $xxx.x.xxx.1xx$.

Earlier work

I suppose a desire to find and understand the pattern of the world about us is built into us, one might say genetically, as a means of survival. To see the possibilities in a situation, even if only to seize a stick for defence, is a fundamental use of the human imagination. To seek a general understanding of how the universe is made seems no more than a development of the problem of seeking a specific understanding of how in time of hunger to catch a fish or attain a fruit which is out of reach. Before the arrival of written records we have no means of knowing what speculation and what insight were achieved by our ancestors; but it is remarkable how soon people set down their views of the world when they had learnt to spell.

From the earliest times we have records of commercial transactions, lists of possessions, codes of laws, letters of command, annals, rituals, royal and religious documents. As soon as a collection of these became large enough, a filing and finding problem appeared. This is still with us. Our methods of solving it form a spectrum whose endpoints are the classification of items and the co-ordinate index. The first of these consists in breaking down the whole range of information with which the collection deals (and this may be coterminous with the whole extent of knowledge) into mutually exclusive and collectively exhaustive sections. The sections are then broken down in a similar way, until a sufficiently large group of sufficiently fine divisions has been achieved. The material to be filed is then placed in position according to its main subject matter, this being the subject represented by one (and only one) of the available divisions. This approach encourages the keeper of the records to put the major sciences, technologies and arts into a suitable order. The choice of order reflects the personal views of the classifier, strongly affected by the informed opinion of his time. This method is of old and respectable lineage.

The second technique is of more recent origin. It consists of making a list of the elements of knowledge and using a search mechanism to bring them together to describe the material sought. This material — books, papers, files, pictures and indeed anything else which is indexed — is stored in any convenient order, generally a numerical order which corresponds to the order in which it was acquired. The elements of knowledge which are used to find it, however, cannot be so treated. They must be given a suitable arrangement. This time, however, the keeper of the records is not faced with a problem of analysing the great kingdom of information into its constituent disciplines. Instead, he or she is concerned with finding positions for notions which are to be used in synthesis.

These elements of knowledge may be stored alphabetically according to their names, so that a sort of dictionary of available search words if formed; or they may be arranged according to any convenient special grouping (for example, the scheme of notions used in an index of personnel records is affected by the administrative needs of the organization concerned); or, lastly, they may be both classified and concerned with a range of knowledge which is wide enough for views on the structure of the world to be brought into play, and put into a suitable, entirely general order. This last situation led to my own investigation of the holotheme.

Although co-ordinate indexing is a recent development, the need to arrange the elements of knowledge in a significant order is old, perhaps even older than the arrangement of major subjects. The First Chapter of Genesis provides an example. First come heaven and earth, light and darkness, sea and land; plants follow; then, in order, come fish, birds and animals of the land; man appears at the end of the sequence. This is not presented in the form 'first came astrophysics and geology, then optics, oceanography and mineralogy, followed by botany, three branches of zoology and anthropology at the end'. It is to do with individual things, not subjects.

Early arrangements of notions reveal a strong drive towards finding an order of importance, generally starting with lowly minerals, and running through the vegetable and animal kingdom to reach mankind, the realm of ideas, and at last the region of the supernatural. This is in general an arrangement according to increasing power, increasing command over environment: materials are inert; plants can do little; animals can do something; mankind can do much, especially with the aid of reason; a god can do everything.

The Greeks

In the West, it is with the Greeks that we first find a new

type of general pattern·proposed. This arises from speculation about how the world is made: it is a constructive
pattern, and as such it is the ancestor of all later studies of
integrative levels. Thales of Miletus held that all things were
forms of the element water, which could become solid to
varying degrees, forming earth and rock, or could pass
through mist to air and so to the even more pure aether and
thus to fire. Anaximenes, somewhat later, chose air as his
elemental substance. Anaximander, between the two, fixed
on an indeterminate substance from which air, water, earth
and fire separated out, and into which, by a sort of
cancellation, they could return. Thus a considerable school of
philosophers, two thousand five hundred years ago, more or
less, began to look at the ultimate structure of things and
selected various types of matter as their starting point.

At the same time, in the same tradition of constructive
pattern, Pythagoras concluded that all things were numbers.
Thus within little more than three generations a division of
view between those who start with physics and those who
start with mathematics became established. This division still
continues to trouble us. For example, the work of the
Classification Research Group, already mentioned, starts with
what is called 'level 1: fundamental particles', placing mathematical notions much later, amongst the mentefacts. My
own analysis, by contrast, follows the views of the Pythagoreans: that is where my investigations led me. As it happened,
the Pythagoreans ran into trouble when they found irrational
numbers (the very name, irrational, is due to them). They
could not accept these, and in consequence found it
impossible to make a neat connection between numbers and
geometry. In the language of holothemics, they failed to
move easily from the set-theoretic to the spatial level.

About three generations after Pythagoras, Zeno studied
mathematical problems and reached a conclusion which,
when I first read of it, led me to compare his work with the
conclusions indicated by the relation code. Zeno was

concerned with comparisons between geometry and arithmetic. He decided, as Burnet puts it (*Greek Philosophy*, London, 1914) that 'geometry cannot be reduced to arithmetic so long as the number one is regarded as the beginning of the numerical series. What really corresponds to the point is what we call zero'. If this remark is translated into the language of the relation code sequences, it amounts to saying that points, in the spatial level, correspond to instances of zero in the set-theoretic level. This is true: the rank and grade sequence of each is 0.000. It used to concern me, a little, that zero appeared in a grade which I knew as the grade of units; but Zeno reassured me.

Water, air and fire (which was Heraclitus' choice for the role of primary material) were all thought of as substances; exactly how they formed the numberless materials of everyday life was not clear. With Leucippus and his disciple Democritus an answer was forthcoming: matter was made of unsplittable atoms, which were arranged in differing patterns according to the substances which they composed. Democritus was still alive, though old, when Plato founded the Academy in Athens. Plato developed a theory which brought together the idea of a small number of different elements (air, water, earth, fire and a rather mysterious fifth), the concept of atoms, and various principles of geometry. These he connected by associating atoms of the various elements with the five regular solids: the triangular pyramid was the shape of the atom of fire; the octohedron was that of the atom of air; the icosahedron was the shape of the atom of water; the cube was that of the atom of earth; and the most refined substance, associated with the farthest boundaries of the universe, had atoms in the shape of dodecahedra. From the viewpoint of holothemics, the interest in this is the connection between the spatial level and the domain of physics. Plato went further: the regular solids can be built up from triangles, and these include the half square whose hypoteneuse is incommensurable with its other two sides. Here is an irrational number of the sort which perturbed the Pythagoreans. Here is a connection with the set-theoretic level. This theory even provides for something akin to chemical reactions: an octohedral atom of air provides enough triangles of the right type to form two atoms of fire.

The progression of levels upward from the physical omitted the cellular: in the absence of the microscope it is hard to see how it could have done otherwise. Aristotle, who studied under Plato and later set up his own school at the Lyceum, was the son of a physician and put great effort into the study of living things, but he could hardly start at a stage lower than that of organs which could be seen on dissection. Lucretius, who lived in Italy some two hundred and fifty years later, wrote (in 'The Nature of the Universe') that 'whatever is seen to be sentient is nevertheless composed of atoms that are insentient', thus emphasizing a view which tied living materials to fundamental unsplittable particles. Such assertions, however, did not go far to explain how inanimate matter was prevailed upon to produce the effects of life and the mind. Aristotle had concluded that a fifth element, the pneuma, was involved, in addition to air and water, earth and fire. One is reminded again of the fifth regular solid. Among the substances formed out of pneuma, there are vegetative, sensitive and rational substances, corresponding to the natural, vital and rational spirits of the Stoics, whose developing system of philosophy lasted for some five hundred years from its beginning shortly after the life of Aristotle. Here again we meet the sequence plant — beast — mankind. Galen, at the end of this period, held this view, and it was passed on to the thinkers of the middle ages.

Mediaeval to modern

The tendency for mathematics to appear first in systematic treatments of knowledge continued and continues today: the present analysis in the language or relation codes is an example. In *Classification and Indexing in Science* (London, second edition, 1959), B.C. Vickery lists more than twenty examples of classifications of the sciences and technologies. They show how these have been viewed, throughout the centuries, as more or less homogeneous blocks of knowledge separated from the whole of human experience and moved about from place to place as may best appeal to the classifier concerned. They also show that, in this selection at least, schemes beginning with mathematics or with logic followed by mathematics outnumber the others by more than two to one. In 1140 Hugh of Saint Victor began with mathematics and geometry; Roger Bacon did the same in 1250. Both these schoolmen also adopted the pattern 'mineral — vegetable — animal' higher in their arrangements. So did nine-tenths of the remainder of the examples. This is a very persistent pattern, and indeed it is perfectly useful even when the classifier regards botany and zoology as equals in the same integrative level or domain.

The principle of the Great Chain of Being, starting with minerals, excelling in durability, followed by plants, excelling in growth, and then by animals, excelling in the bodily senses, and then by mankind, whose excellence is reason, is clearly stated in E.M.W. Tillyard's *The Elizabethan World Picture* (London, 1943). The scheme continues through nine ranks of angels to the Deity. The reign of Elizabeth I just entered the seventeenth century; it was about two thousand years since Plato's day. During all this period there was no increase in knowledge sufficient to make any major change in either approach to the arrangement of ideas — the classification of main subjects or the finding of a sequence in the chain of individual objects. Object sequences continued to suggest subject sequences to writers of encyclopaedias and other accounts of the world. They still do. Uses for object sequences, however, were few.

During the next two hundred years, this situation was to change. Many philosophers and scientists, trapped in their own languages after the decline in the use of Latin, felt the need for developing a new universal speech for use in international learned discourse. This need was felt even by those who still wrote in Latin themselves. Among those who were attracted by the idea, Francis Bacon, Newton, Descartes, Leibniz and Wilkins may be mentioned. A universal language demanded an arrangement of notions which imitated reality with sufficient precision to be a reliable basis for the new tongue. In 1668, Wilkins tried to meet this need with his *Essay towards a Real Character and a Philosophical Language.* This contained a remarkable arrangement of ideas covering an immense range of knowledge. In passing, it incorporated the ubiquitous mineral — vegetable — animal sequence. Wilkins included qualities, actions and relations, together with much about the mind. At the foot of each branch of his classification of notions, a set of synonyms or closely related words is found.

Nearly two hundred years later than the *Essay*, in 1852, Peter Mark Roget published his *Thesaurus of English Words and Phrases.* He had been working on it since about 1805. Like the work of Wilkins, it is an arrangement of notions, round each of which a collection of related words is clustered. In his introduction, Roget mentions various purposes his work might serve, including the standardization of the English tongue, the forming of a polyglot lexicon by using the *Thesaurus* to arrange words in other languages, the analysis of ideas, and the development of a universal or philosophic speech with a view to removing the barriers of communication between the different nations to mankind. These are all secondary purposes, however. The principal aim is to provide a pattern of ideas in which similar notions are brought together, as an aid to literary composition.

Roget starts his work with abstract relations and number, followed by space, inorganic matter, plants and animals and mankind. Then he travels through sensations, the intellect, the communication of ideas and individual and social volition, where many concepts of the communal and national level are found. He then proceeds through personal, sympathetic and moral affections to a concluding section on religion: superhuman beings, doctrines, sentiments, acts and institutions. The arrangement is so effective that when it was revised more than a century after its first appearance its new editor reported that some fifty thousand new entries had been made in it without destroying its framework, which was still both workable and comprehensive. At the time of its first publication, Boole's *Laws of Thought* and John Newland's law of octaves for the chemical elements were still two years in the future. Seven years were to pass before Darwin published his *Origin of Species*, twelve before Mendeleev produced his periodic table, nineteen before Rutherford, who split the atom, was born.

During the second half of the nineteenth century (starting, by a co-incidence, in 1852) Herbert Spencer began to put forward an early theory of integrative levels based on the idea of progressive movement from the simple to the complex: evolution under its most general aspect. In *First Principles* (London, sixth edition, 1900), now fortified by the work of Darwin and Wallace, he gave as examples the development of the earth from a hot ball of gases, the differentiation of plants and animals from simpler ancestors, and the development of supranational bodies out of nations. He emphasized that society is an organism, comparing it — and contrasting it — with the individual animal. This aspect of the matter is shown well by the relation code sequences: the very pattern of units and zeros in the codes for the cytomechanic and biomorphic levels is to be found embedded in the code patterns of the communal and the national. It is easy to treat a road system and a cardiovascular system as serving a similar purpose at different levels; the same applies to a telephone system and a nervous system.

This use of the concept of evolution as a tool to produce an ordering of notions comes close to present-day views on integrative levels. Above the grade of the photon, at least, it seems that more complex entities and attributes have appeared — indeed, could not help but appear — later than simpler ones. Though the realization of this has led to some dimensional fallacies (as already mentioned) the fact of a general movement seems to be certain.

Some thirty years younger than Spencer, Melvil Dewey came to the problem of arranging knowledge from the side of the practical librarian. His approach was that of the classifier: knowledge was divided into ten main classes — generalia, philosophy, religion, sociology, linguistics, pure science, applied science, recreation, literature and history. The first edition of the Decimal Classification which he created appeared in 1876. It was too early for sufficient knowledge to have been amassed for a full statement of integrative levels to be worked out; and even if this had been available there is no assurance that it would have been adopted as a means of producing subject order. Whether, and (if so) how, to use integrative levels for this purpose has not yet been determined, and may have to await a wider understanding of the pattern which is now appearing. At any rate, within the small section allotted to the sciences, something like a series of levels appears in Dewey's work: mathematics is followed by astronomy and physics; chemistry and earth sciences come next; then after palaeontology come the biological sciences — botany first, zoology next. Applied sciences, which form the next main class, may be thought of as mainly concerned with industrial and commercial activities at the communal level; much the same may be said of recreation except that here we are concerned with leisure-time activities. The class concerned with literature would, in relation-code parlance, be found largely in the class of special ideas. The social sciences, in the highest domain in the mundane class of notions, are placed before pure sciences and languages by Dewey: the present holothemic analysis would place most of them (for example, political science, economics, law, public administration) above the communal (industrial, commercial, recreational) studies.

With the advent of the twentieth century, the contrast between an order of subjects and an order of elementary notions became a matter for study. Brian Vickery, in the work already quoted, comments on the lectures of Richardson (1901, but the reference is to E.C. Richardson, *Classification, Theoretical and Practical*, New York, 3rd edition, 1930). Richardson remarked that 'the order of the sciences is the order of things', and made it clear that by 'things' he meant objects, activities, qualities, ideas and, it seems, in general all the sorts of term and relation here called 'semantic types'. He pursued the matter of arranging things, defined thus comprehensively, and gave in essence a series of levels beginning with that of sub-atomic particles and proceeding through molecules and cells to men and societies. He held the view that to classify subjects rather than objects was 'a profound theoretical and practical mistake, leading to endless confusion'. Certainly anything can be a subject, and can then reach forward and backward through the holotheme until its boundaries are lost and it is tangled with every other subject in the book. Let us make a science: first, write a word down at random; next, add the suffix 'ology'; behold, a subject is born.

Interest in the constructive order of notions becomes more and more apparent as work on organizing knowledge proceeds in the twentieth century. The actual name, 'integrative level', does not seem to have been used before 1937, when Joseph Needham introduced it in his Herbert Spencer Lecture at Oxford, which was entitled 'Integrative Levels: a Revaluation of the Idea of Progress'. This is printed in his book, *Time, the Refreshing River* (London, 1943). Needham mentions just one earlier use of the word 'level' in this context (S. Alexander's *Space, Time and Deity*, London, 1927). Much of his article deals with the rightness of Spencer's views on the organization of society. He relates these to the existence of a level concerned with nations, discussing improved internal national structures and the development of higher forms of society which bring nations together — that is, discussing the contents of the higher rank of the national level. Towards the end of his account, he restates the 'giant vista of evolution', in particular noting the parallel development of plants and animals and referring to mind as 'a phenomenon of high organizational level'. Here he agrees, even in the wording chosen, with the placing of mind as a phenomenon in a high position (though not, of course, the highest).

So brief an account of the precursors of the relation-code approach to the holotheme must be supplemented. Stephen Toulmin and June Goodfield's *The Architecture of Matter* (London, 1962) contains a thorough survey of views and inquiries about how the world is made, from the practical wisdom of an ancient craftsmen to the conclusions of the present day. Its epilogue expresses the authors' view: 'The most far-reaching outcome we can hope for from twentieth-century matter-theory — which includes both quantum mechanics and molecular biology, as well as half a dozen other specialities — is a common system of fundamental concepts, embracing material systems at every level.' In my more hopeful moments I like to think that the relation code system, based on arranging ideas according to their structure, may turn out to be such a unifying instrument.

Co-ordinate indexing

The principles of a co-ordinate index have already been described, and we have seen that if such an index is designed for handling documents with a wide range of subject-matter then its thesaurus (its collection of elements of knowledge) must be equally wide. The relation code principle can be used as a basis for such an extensive thesaurus, either as it stands or as a hidden classification of notions governing the relations between ideas, when these are recorded in the retrieval mechanism in alphabetic order of the names they are given. In practice, most thesauri used for this purpose are alphabetic, so a means of relating the ideas is most helpful. It is remarkable how far asunder the alphabet can place related notions.

There are many reasons for recording the connections between ideas in such a list. For example, the troubles caused by the existence of synonyms and homonyms must be overcome; proper relations between words of broader and narrower meaning must be established, and means of building up more complex notions from those of the simpler sort must be made safe. In the absence of proper knowledge of how to assemble ideas, they may combine in undesirable ways and lead the index to find documents which do not satisfy the search questions. It was work on problems of this nature which first led me to study and identify the senantic types. It led me to the distinction between generics and collectives, and it provided me with an approach to the definition of integrative levels and formative stages by noting the limits of semantic factoring.

Semantic factoring (known to linguists as componential analysis) can be well shown by means of an example. Consider the notion 'schoolgirl'. This can be analysed into the notions 'juvenile', 'human', 'feminine' and 'pupillary'. The first three of these make up the notion 'girl', which is not quite as specific as 'schoolgirl'. The first two form 'child', which is even less specific. To add 'pupillary' to this is to form 'schoolchild', a notion which has the same degree of specificity as 'girl'.

If it is carried far enough, semantic factoring leads to the recovery of notions which cannot be further factored. At this point, dictionaries tend to rely on synonyms ('Juvenile: young', says the Concise Oxford). Encyclopaedias may try the sort of ostensive definition which provides a picture of the thing (or other term) concerned. In addition, or alternatively, they may try verbal description; but this leads to circular definition if it is not made up entirely of notions of a lower grade than the one defined. In fact, to keep a definition sequence in being, directed uniformly from the simple to the complex, constructive descriptions are unavoidable once the most general ideas in a stage have been factored out from the more complicated.

Many co-ordinate indexes do not handle subject matter, but directly index objects or events — chemicals, machines, people, places, accidents, sales, illnesses, deliveries of goods. The work of framing classified lists of features for use in these was another source of information about semantic types. It showed the distinction between passive entities such as chemicals, machines, people and places, which were described by passive features — qualities — and active entities such as accidents, sales, illnesses and deliveries, whose descriptors were active features — modes. When features of the sort used in these indexes were used in thesauri as elements of subject matter they did not change their behaviour. Experience of their use in both varieties of index lay behind their appearance in the relation code sequences which formalize the full pattern of the holotheme.

It is instructive to see how a co-ordinate index which directly relates items to their features, may be absorbed into an index of the topics treated in a document. The items and the features, together with the connections between them, form what is known as a data field. Such a field may be very complicated, containing much information about intricate matters, and of course it is described in words — the words which are candidates for inclusion in the thesaurus of notions which may be used as an aid to search. Indeed, the subject matter of any document is a data field or a linked set of these, and when the document becomes an item in a co-ordinate index then the items in its included fields of textual matter become features of its contents, recorded against it. Their change of status is signified by the use of the word 'about'. An index of objects may record, against the item known as the sky, the feature that it is blue. An index of documents may record, against the item known as the document concerned, the features that it is about the sky and about blueness. Much of the trouble encountered by those who apply co-ordinate indexing to textual matter arises because an essentially two-dimensional pattern is thus compressed into a single dimension under the item, the document, to which it belongs.

Data fields

The behaviour of a data field can be examined by putting marks at the places where its items (represented by rows or columns) cross its features (represented by columns or rows). Signals of this sort make it clear which items have which features. Each item is revealed as a member of many different subsets of the full set of features, while each feature is a member of many different subsets of the full set of items. All the numerical and set-theoretic relations of the lowest integrative level may be shown by the use of such a field (it is, of course, a field in the strict mathematical sense), and this is yet another source of the remarkable contribution made by co-ordinate indexing to the theory of integrative levels. It exhibited the pattern of the ground level. Indeed, the reason why a data field, embodied in a computer memory or a set of punched feature cards or in a flat tray visible index or any other device, may represent any collection of notions whatever, is now clear. The relation pattern of the lowest integrative level, to which its data field behaviour corresponds, is embodied in the pattern of all higher levels.

The operations and conditions of the lower rank of this lowest level can all be demonstrated by the use of a data field diagram without using any subsets which are transverse to each other. Since items can be treated as subsets of the full set of features, while features can be treated as subsets of the

FIGURE 6: A simple field of five items and six features. Another example is analysed more extensively in Appendix A

To help relate the data field to everyday life, the items may be thought of as plants and animals, according to the following scheme:

(items)		(features)	
0 : crow		A : animal kingdom
1 : canary		B : plant kingdom
2 : Brimstone butterfly		C : bird
		D : insect
3 : buttercup		E : yellow
4 : snowdrop		F : corvine

Under this scheme a blob at the intersection of row 3 with column E indicates that the buttercup is yellow.

	A	B	C	D	E	F
0	●		●			●
1	●		●		●	
2	●			●	●	
3		●			●	
4		●				

In a data field a feature is recognisable as a subset of items: thus the subset 0, 1, 2 (shown as three blobs in column A) represents feature A. (This of course leaves any knowledge obtained from sources *outside* the field out of account.)

As an example of a set-theoretic condition found in the field, the condition of containing may be taken. Feature A contains feature C which contains feature F, as may be seen by inspection.

full set of items, either dimension of the field may be used. Appendix A gives an example. The usual procedure is to consider the full set of items and to examine the subsets of items (which all, in the diagram, lie parallel to each other). Thus one subset may be shown to include another, to overlap another, to be identical with another. The condition of membership, however, cannot be shown in this way. It is a transversive condition, as already mentioned, and it calls for the use of two mutually transverse subsets if it is to be demonstrated. It is found at the start of the higher rank of the level, being a between-set (as opposed to a within-set) relation. On the attributive side, multiplication is a typical transversive or between-set relation. In a data field it appears as an operation upon two sets or subsets of which one is taken from one dimension of the field while the other is taken from the other. The result of the multiplication is the number of connections, crossings, between the members of one set or subset and the members of the other. These crossings carry the marks, standing for data units, to show whether or not the item concerned has the feature which crosses it at that point. Thus the multiplication together of the natural numbers of the two sets which make a data field produces the number of data units it contains.

In passing, it may be noted that the condition of membership (the first transverse condition in the series of conditions of set theory) is irreflexive. This has a bearing on Russell's famous paradox. The paradox runs as follows: 'Consider the set of all sets which are not members of themselves: if it is a member of itself, then it is not a member of itself; and if it is not a member of itself, then it must be a member of itself.' However, since membership is irreflexive, no set is a member of itself, and in consequence the paradox does no more than ask us to consider the set of all sets. We cannot then suppose this set to be a member of itself, owing to the properties of membership; and if we think of it as finite, then we must suppose either that it is not a set or that it goes against the rules. Sticking to the irreflexive property of membership, we conclude that the set of all sets is infinite. The paradox reduces to: 'Consider the set of all sets: it is infinite.' So it is, and so is the number of all whole numbers. Reference to the relation code sequences of the set-theoretic level shows that fractionality is the attributive analogue of membership. Substituting attributive for entitive throughout the paradox, we obtain: 'Consider the whole number of all whole numbers which are not fractions of themselves: if it is a fraction of itself, then it is not a fraction of itself, and if it is not a fraction of itself, then it must be a fraction of itself.' Here, also, the first supposition is impossible (owing to the irreflexive property of fractionality) while the second supposition amounts to: 'Since it is whole, it must be counted as part of the total which it makes.' This in turn leads to the conclusion that it is infinite.

Applications

The need to solve certain problems in co-ordinate indexing provided the impetus to start the work which ended with the development of the relation code sequences. The problems were quite large in number, ranging from semantic factoring, already mentioned, to the representation of part-to-whole, constituent-to-whole, and activity-to-purpose relations. There are advantages in being able to distinguish between clay-for-bricks-for-walls-for-houses-for-towns, clay-brick-walled-houses-for-towns, towns-with-houses-with-walls-of-bricks-of-clay, and similar search requirements in which the same notions appear in different orders and disguises. In this example, the principal notion of the first series of ideas is 'clay'; that of the second is 'houses'; that of the third is 'towns'. If an indication of the level of the principal notion can be given, then lower notions become adjectival, referring to its construction, and higher notions can be seen to refer to its use. If such an indicator cannot be used, then (since all ideas in a co-ordinate index are independent) the concepts will be unanchored and will drift into all sorts of wrong arrangements.

Another problem arises from the way in which translation (say, from English to French) alters the order in which notions are placed in any alphabetic thesaurus. Fortunately, change of language does not affect relation code sequences. Julius Caesar is to be found somewhere in position 0.101.1.000.011, or 05103, in any tongue. Yet another concern of the co-ordinate indexer is to seek an assurance that no important notion is omitted from the thesaurus, and that effective definitions are available, to aid understanding and to control the secular drift of meaning which occurs to words as customs change and personalities alter. Regular schemes for defining ideas are valuable here.

The notions used in a co-ordinate index may be of any degree of complexity. There is nothing in principle to stop the indexer using such a concept as 'the effect of gift stamp trading on the profit ratio of all-night automobile service stations', nor is there anything to stop languages developing single words for such ideas. In supplying rules for constructing and positioning complicated notions of this kind, the holothemic pattern may provide a service for subject classifications of the analytic type. Large numbers of subject arrangements break down the field of knowledge into ideas of at least this degree of complexity. The rules for forming such notions, permuting their elements, work on the relation codes, though subject classifications are very different from co-ordinate indexes.

In the realm of mathematics the relation code sequences may have many applications. They appear to form a remarkably neat classification of that subject; and, if this is so, they may offer clues both to the solution of special problems and to the teaching of the subject as a whole. For example, a textbook on set and number theory could be patterned on the relation code sequences. Such a work might also help to tidy up some of the present nomenclature of the discipline: for example, what is here called a condition is called a relation in most mathematical textbooks, with the result that the mathematician is left with no word to cover both together.

The relation code sequences may have even wider application than is found in mathematics if they are examined in the context of the whole school and university curriculum. The holothemic pattern is a map of knowledge. As interdisciplinary studies grow in importance and as schools develop the techniques of project work in which their pupils are assisted by resource centres, the older divisions between subjects become blurred. Then a new set of guidelines is needed to replace the vanishing boundaries. The framework of levels and grades may well serve such a purpose. If it proves valid, it will remain firm no matter how the temporary partitions within it are arranged and rearranged to suit academic needs.

I recall a simple example of this application of guidelines in the realm of curriculum development. It is possible to divide the subjects taught at the average school for teenagers into those which involve physical and mental skills — woodwork, languages, trigonometry, swimming — and those which are concerned with describing a pattern — the organization of government, the sequence of history, the structure of the atom, the construction of the human body. Obviously the two types overlap: languages involve patterns of grammar, the study of biology involves handling a microscope. However, if the largely descriptive element of education is considered on its own, it may be compared, subject by subject, with the levels of the holotheme. This is a revealing exercise. When I carried it out in respect of my own children I found that their schooling dealt with the structure of things at every level except the communal. Sets and shapes were dealt with by mathematics, particles, atoms and molecules by physics or chemistry, cells and living beings by biology, and the structure of government both national and local by various combinations of history, civics and current affairs. By contrast, the structure of any large administrative body below that of local government was conspicuously absent. It was no teacher's duty to explain that an industrial company has a quality control section, a cash flow system, a maintenance department, a time office, besides the more obvious production lines and sales offices. Companies, clubs, professional associations and other main units of the communal level, with their departmental sub-units, were omitted, or dealt with only by the way in connection with other subjects. Incidentally, I suspect that a very useful analysis of management science could be based on the layout of the communal level. So far as the school curriculum is concerned, I concluded that in my children's case the organizations in which they are most likely to earn their livings are the ones least likely to have been explained to them, even by the harassed and probably press-ganged careers adviser.

The pattern of the holotheme may be of use in linguistics also. If it is the business of language to imitate things as they are, and if the pattern corresponds well with reality, then the student of language may learn much from the code, and the student of the code may learn much from the behaviour of languages. It may turn out that the binary pattern I describe can act as a neutral reference against which the codes we know as languages may be measured. The question may come to be, how does this or that type of speech imitate the arrangement of notions in the holotheme? What does it omit? What does it alter? How are its nouns, adjectives and verbs related to entities, attributes, operations?

Most especially, the relation code appeals to me as a unifying device, an arrangement of the elements of knowledge which in fact possesses the desirable properties I listed at the start. It is infinitely hospitable: every place in it can be subdivided as necessary. It is easily taught: although it contains much that is new, there are no great difficulties in learning the binary pattern it embodies or the classes, domains, levels, ranks and the like which it contains.

Although the properties of relations may not be common knowledge to all today, our schools are introducing work on set theory in the new mathematics, and laying a foundation upon which the series of integrative levels may in time come to seem a natural edifice. It is independent of personal opinion: given the rules, an Arabic-speaking Eskimo living in Peru will, from standard textbooks, place the concepts of photosynthesis, Tarzan of the Apes, the omega minus particle and the acceleration of derived demand in the same positions as will a Bantu-speaking Russian in Bengal: not because he or she has referred to the schedules or the decisions of a central authority but because that is where the notions fit. It is based on a simple repetitive pattern: little is simpler than binary, and binary is certainly widely-known. Perhaps I should add that the binary pattern came of itself during my inquiry. I started out with no sort of idea as to what I might find. If I had begun sixty years ago, when little was known of set-theory or the contents of the subatomic level or the things to be found inside a living cell I should have had a harder time of it, and might well have ended in boredom or despair turning to the attractions of chess or politics or fishing. I was fortunate in my decade, which gave me the materials for the work, and in my family, who allowed me to play with symbols when I should have been mowing the lawn, and in my local authority, whose many public libraries provided me with books by the dozen.

Conclusion

When I look at this whole structure of thought I realize how much of it has been found or checked by the process of comparison. If a gap is found in the operations on subsets, it may be filled by comparison with the operations on numbers (supposing these to be known) at the same grade and level. Other, more distant comparisons are to be found also. I remember seeing a film on television, made by time-lapse photography, which had the strange effect of showing people in the guise of a substance, seemingly pumped by regular pulses across roads controlled by traffic lights, dispersing on leaving the entrances to subways, drawn from all quarters to the gates of stadia by an unseen force. It seemed that the city breathed them as a lung breathes molecules of the substances in air. For amusement, I checked the integrative levels. The number of grades between a city and its people is exactly the same as the number between a lung and its air! I thought: the city breathing people in and out: what a tremendous poetic image. I was often one of those people in the city of London. I knew how the unhappy and the frustrated might feel in the presence of this huge impartial simile. Yet it is no criticism of modern life. Time-lapse photography of the migration of peoples in the nomadic days when northern Europe was swamp and forest would have shown exactly the same effect. There is an exciting literary study to be carried out on the similarities of the levels. It is so like the doctrine of correspondences, macrocosm and microcosm, of the first Elizabethan days: in principle, at least. As individuals, we belong to neither: we inhabit a mesocosm from which the view is vast in all directions.

The connection between a city and its people, a lung and its air, leads to another: can a sort of slide rule be made, graduated with operations (for example, those of mathematics) in their holothemic order, so that the holotheme may be displaced in relation to itself just as a slide rule displaces a scale of numbers? Such an arrangement could have put the city opposite to the lung, allowing 'people' to be read off against 'air'. If the operations of mathematics were recorded on the slide in this way, the unit grade could be set anywhere along the holothemic series, and higher grades would then have their appropriate mathematics in register against them, on the assumption that the notions opposite the origin were to be taken as units for the purpose in hand. This would certainly put mathematical group theory correctly opposite to the omega minus particle whose existence it predicted, the flow of traffic · opposite to liquid flow, money against energy (and indeed, money is well treated as social energy) — all for suitable displacements of the pattern.

However attractive this course of speculation may be, it is probably time to stop. Once more a summary may be useful.

Since about the middle of the twentieth century there has been a considerable growth of interest in the question of levels of integration: What levels exist, and how are they related to each other? At the same time, the development of the major sciences has reached a point at which answers to these questions appear to be possible. If it is compared with the relation code approach, other work in this field seems to introduce unnecessary complexity, arising mainly from two enticing but mistaken views: an attempt to found a level on the mind, and perhaps to incorporate mathematics and other abstractions into this in the guise of mentefacts; and an attempt to found a series of levels on spatial or temporal dimensions. All this has been done in the course of a conscious search for constructive pattern, but without making use of the science of pattern: set and number theory.

The present effort is but the most recent manifestation of a very old study. The history of this displays two lines of development, each of two strands. The search for an arrangement of notions according to their structure stems from the work of the Greeks two thousand or more years ago; the search for an arrangement based on their importance, as measured by their real or imaginary power, stems from an even older source: it is to be found as far back as we can descry. Both methods have been applied in two ways: to break down the field of knowledge into subjects, and to arrange single ideas — the elements of knowledge — in order. When attempts are made to use a constructive order for the elements of knowledge it becomes possible to seek laws relating integrative levels to each other; the development of such laws may be expected to lead to valuable results in many different fields. These include co-ordinate indexing, from which a great deal of the present research has sprung; they also include linguistics, mathematics, educational technology and possibly other sciences and technologies where patterns are of especial significance.

The set of relation code sequences has the useful properties of being infinitely hospitable, easily taught, simple in its essence and independent of personal opinion. The method used for forming it can be applied by all who care to try it: the same order of major types of idea will always result. It is this replicability which distinguishes it from other schemes for organizing knowledge. It may perhaps appear too cut and dried, too facile, too pat an answer, in comparison with the xtraordinary richness and diversity of the universe we inhabit: its very regularities may make it seem hard to accept. Yet consider the deeps and the abstruse complexities of mathematics, the nested patterns of numbers, natural, rational, real and complex, each moving out to infinity — four passages to infinity even before that great domain is conquered. Then reflect that this is but the groundwork. Beyond lies the realm of physics; and beyond this again lies that of the life sciences; and beyond these lie the social sciences; and even this is no more than part of the land to be explored. For above the class of all mundane ideas there stretches the class of special notions, comprehended by the imagination, interpreting the mundane for recreation, guidance, insight, understanding. This is the vista which opens from our simple binary pattern. For me, this simplicity is wealth enough.

Appendix A

A DATA FIELD AND ITS CONTENTS

The following is a typical diagram of a data field, as used in the course of lectures on indexing to audiences drawn from such widely differing disciplines as medicine, personnel administration, librarianship, organization and methods work, teaching and engineering. In all these cases and in many others the problems of recording information for later retrieval and processing arise. When lecturing on such a topic, the items and features of the field are given particular names to correspond with the familiar activities of the audience. Here they are simply represented by letters (for the features) and numerals (for the items). The reader may find it helpful to think of the items as people and of the features as their characteristics: for example, artful, bashful, cheerful, dark, energetic and feminine.

In the field, a blob is used to indicate that an item possesses a feature. Thus each column of such marks indicates the particular subset of the full set of items which possesses the feature represented by the column. Six subsets are shown, corresponding to the six features: clearly, others are possible if the field is extended. Similarly, each row shows the subset of the full set of features which is possessed by the item represented by the row. Thus the relations which are found between subsets, within full sets, can be shown by using either dimension of the field. Relations between full sets are transversive, and can only be shown by using both dimensions.

Here is the sample field:

←——————— FEATURES ———————→

	A	B	C	D	E	F
0	●		●			
1	●	●	●	●		●
2					●	
3	●	●				●
4		●			●	
5	●		●	●		●

ITEMS (vertical axis)

The relation code sequences described in Chapter 2 were developed as a result of studying the properties of the operations and conditions to be found in such a field as this. The following are examples of the relations concerned:

disjunction : subsets *A* and *E* are disjoint (note how the subsets of items are named by the use of their defining features). In the other dimension, subsets 1 and 2 are disjoint. Other examples of disjunction can be found in the field.

containing : subset *A* contains subset *C*, which contains subset *D*; in the other dimension subset 1 contains subset 5 which contains subset 0.

overlap : subset *B* overlaps subset *C*; subset 0 overlaps subset 3. Other examples of overlap are to be found; these two instances show every possibility (the members of the full set may appear in both, either, or neither of the subsets).

intersection : the intersection of subset C with subset F is subset D.

addition : the natural number of subset A is 4 (it has four members); that of subset E is 2; the addition of the two is 6, the number of members in the full set concerned. Note that this works because the two subsets are disjoint.

subtraction : the natural number of A is 4; and that of C is 3; and the result of subtracting 3 from 4 is 1, the number of members in the larger subset (A) which are not in the smaller (C). Note that this works because A contains C.

membership : unlike the preceding examples, this relation cannot be shown without using both dimensions of the field: it is transversive. Item 3 is a member of subset B (we may say, item 3 is a member of feature B, or subset 3 is a member of subset B, or even 'person 3 is bashful' or 'bashful is person 3', which is poetic, like 'blue was the sea').

multiplication : if we multiply the number of items, 6, by the number of features, 6, we obtain the number of cells, crossings or data units in the field: 36. Here again two dimensions are employed: multiplication is transversive.

These examples could be extended in many ways, but this is sufficient to demonstrate the source of some of the methods used for exploring the set-theoretic level.

Appendix B

EXAMPLES OF PLACEMENT

The following few notions have been defined very briefly and given code sequences according to the relation code pattern, as further examples of the method. There is a great deal to be learnt about it still. Problems arise even when the indexer is concerned with apparently simple ideas – for example, the concept of a trade name, or a googly, or a sundowner (either meaning), or stamp trading, or the Impressionist Movement. Generally the difficulties appear because some ideas are multiple collectives. However, there seems to be no reason why rules for arranging the elements of such notions may not be agreed: a typical rule would be to place these in holothemic order – number before dimension (and, within dimension, space before time), energy before matter, and so on up the scale. Meanwhile, here are some uncomplicated instances.

A MERGER : The merging of two or more organizations to form a single new organization.

The notion is mundane, between such organizations as industrial companies and consequently in the communal level, upper rank. It is not dissociative, it is commutative, it is idempotent (a company is always merged with itself). It is an active entitive term, a phenomenon. Its relation code sequence is therefore 0.110.1.011.111, or 06137 in octal.

A RAINWATER SYSTEM: A series of single-piece parts such as gutters, swan-necks, downspouts and the like, channelling rainwater from the roof of a building to a drain or soakaway. This is not a system in the relation code sense.

The notion is mundane, between single-piece parts without movement, and consequently is in the cyto-mechanic level, lower rank. It is a series and is consequently transitive, not symmetric and not reflex-ive. It is a passive entitive term, a thing. Its relation code sequence is therefore 0.100.0.100.011, or 04043 in octal.

CAUSALITY : Being-a-cause-of. There are many variants: here we take being-an-immediate-physical-cause-of.

The notion is mundane, occurring as soon as energy is available at the sub-atomic level, lower rank. Being immediate, transitivity is irrelevant; it is not symmetric and it is not reflexive (no notion is a cause of itself). It is passive, as opposed to the operation of causing, which is active. It is entitive and it is a relation. Its relation code sequence is therefore 0.010.0.000.010, or 02002 in octal.

Another method of placing ideas displays the relation code sequence step by step as it is built up, thus:

UTOPIA : An imaginary country.

    1 : special
      111 : national level
       1 : upper rank, concerned with entire nations
       000 : a unit within this rank

011 : a thing
1.111.1.000.011 or, in octal, 17103.

PHOTOSYNTHESIS : Formation of complex substances
out of water and carbon dioxide, by the aid of
chlorophyll acted on by light

0 : mundane
  011 : molecular level
   1 : upper rank (requiring molecules)
    101 : a serial process
     111 : a phenomenon
0.011.1.101.111 or, in octal, 03157

There is obviously a great deal of room for discussion,
argument and disagreement in defining and placing ideas. For
example, in the notion 'blue' to be regarded as a quality of
materials (at molecular level) or as a phenomenon, the
vibration of photons (at subatomic level)? It is clearly
possible to accept both meanings. When divergent views
appear on matters of this sort it is generally possible to
accept both, because in practice they simply point out
different meanings for the same word. Deeper philosophic
differences may be found, however, when mental feelings,
emotions, sensations and the like are given homes, as ideas, in
the brain at the lower biomorphic rank. People with an
especially strong belief in the existence of a mental level may
find it hard to co-operate with the relation code pattern to
the extent of treating an idea as a pattern of states in a group
of cells in the brain (or as something similar — here again we
trespass on the very boundaries of knowledge).

For my part, I am willing to pretend that the pattern is
right, and to try to fill it in, as far as is possible, so as to see
what it looks like when it is well supplied with properly
placed ideas. The pretence is easy because in many regions of
the holotheme — in mathematics, for instance — I think it is

right in fact and not in pretence alone. Others may be less sure; but however we feel, it is only by going along with it for a while that we can learn enough about it to judge it fairly. I have the impression that, to an even greater extent than is normal in work with ideas, the examination of the relation code pattern will call for careful study of the arts and sciences concerned. What this will reveal, in the end, who knows? At any rate, we shall all be remarkably well informed.

Appendix C

PREVIOUS NOTES ON THE LEVELS

My inquiry into the pattern of integrative levels has been a long-drawn-out affair with few progress reports. In December 1964 the *Journal of Documentation* published a letter of mine in which I described the general pattern of four major domains and eight levels, together with the chain of types of notion running upward from units through assemblies and higher grades of notion till more advanced units appear. At that time I used the name 'system' for what I now think of as a 'series', and 'combine' for what now seems best named a 'system'. Also, I used names (for some of the semantic types) which differ from those used in the main text of this book. Otherwise, there is little fundamental difference between the pattern then put forward and that of the holotheme as I now see it. Here is the letter:

Dear Sirs,
'Integrative Levels'
I was pleased to see a reference, on pages 157 and 158 of your last issue (September 1964), to work I have been carrying out on the subject of integrative levels and semantic types. The reference appears as part of the Classification Research Group's Bulletin No. 8. It gives provisional lists of levels and types, presented to the Group as work in progress. I should not like to think that any of your readers might now take these and try to build on them, because most of the ideas they contain have failed to prove themselves in practice. Only the set of integrative levels from the cellular to the national remains resistant to my attempts to prove it ill-chosen.

From my own point of view, however, the lists have done their job well. They have made it possible to formulate rules for the detection of integrative levels and for the ways in which a higher level may be built up from a lower. Also, they have made it possible to produce a theory of semantic types which is far more internally consistent than the hypothesis underlying the provisional work.

Your readers can probably see for themselves many of the insufficiencies of the lists. Point-events, for instance, are nor fundamental, since to discuss them we need many specialized ideas — for example, those of set theory, which are therefore earlier.

This is not to say that the ideas given in the lists are not ideas for which we must find places. The point is that they do not seem to be related to each other in the way the lists indicate. Their relations are at the same time more complex (there are more semantic types than those which are given) and more simple (their pattern is more systematic than the lists appear to show).

It is perhaps unfair to pull down earlier work without offering a replacement. My present view is that the list of integrative levels ought to run more like this than like the provisional one:

1. set-theoretic, logical
2. spatial, geometric   logic and mathematics
3. subatomic
4. atomic and molecular   physics and chemistry
5. cellular
6. biomorphic   biology and artefacts
7. communal
8. national   social sciences

Also, it seems to me that the type-structures (for example, atoms, cells, people) of one level come together to form those of the next by a more or less regular chain which can be summarized:

    unit (the type-structure)
    assembly (several, acting together)
    system (several, acting serially)
    combine (several, acting serially with feedback)
    subunit of next level ('organ') ('interlevel')
    assembly (of organs)
    system (of organs)
    combine (of organs)
    unit (the type-structure of the next level)

Possible examples of this are: a mitochondrion is an organ of a cell, defining an interlevel; a flower is an organ of a plant: a personnel department is an organ of a company; the circulatory system is a system of an animal; the road system is a system of a nation; a molecule is an assembly of atoms.

This arrangement is, of course, as much at risk as the original lists whose collapse led to it.

Finally, it appears to me that there are four simple semantic types at each level: things, qualities, changes, and activities. These are so related that any three will define the fourth (as, in another case, energy is defined by mass, length, and time). An example is wind (an activity), which is air (a thing) altering (a change) its position (a quality). At some levels, the word 'phenomenon' may seem more appropriate than 'activity'; but it seems best to choose one name and stick to it.

These four simple types may exist on their own, or may form collections, acting as means of grouping each other — as plastics are things grouped according to a quality, and antiseptics are things grouped according to an activity (as are butchers, bakers, and candle-stick-makers).

Qualities, activities, and changes work up from level to level just as things do. Work study officers spend some of their time breaking down complex activities into their constituent units; and anyone who has drawn a graph has turned unit readings on scales into systems and combines.

These four types, at each level, may aggregate boundlessly to form substances (such as yeast or copper) or they may remain in the form of structures (yeast cells, copper atoms). The distinction between structure and substance also occurs in the case of qualities, changes, and activities. For instance, it occurs in the realm of qualities in the form of a distinction between those which are divisible (such as length) and those which are not (such as position: one cannot have half the North Pole as a definition of a spot on the face of the earth). In the sphere of activities a similar contrast can be made between events and processes.

One of the difficulties of looking at this subject is the fact that words work most efficiently when dealing with complicated meanings. The word 'boy' stands for a double collective of structure: a human being (the structure) distinguished as both masculine and young. In general, the older an art or a craft, the more complex its apparently simple words turn out to be. Moreover, words are like chameleons: they take on protective coloration. Concentrating on meanings, having formed habits of thinking with words, is not easy and one may easily fail.

In addition, discovering a pattern calls as much for a recognition of similarities as it does of differences; this, again, is difficult, since on the whole mankind has survived to date by noticing differences.

For these reasons, I shall be surprised if the analysis I have given above turns out to be correct in all its essential details (I shall also be rather pleased). At the same time, I think it is nearer the truth than was the original report to the Classification Research Group, perhaps by a considerable way. It is, at any rate, sufficiently different for me to feel it should be given as wide a circulation as the earlier and cruder version.

I hope you will forgive so long a letter.

Yours faithfully,
J.L. JOLLEY

Almost all this analysis held good, so far as I could tell, when I continued with my study. During the next few months, the principal change in the pattern was a straightforward addition to it: the four semantic types became eight when the four categories of relation were catered for. This led to the development of the binary triads for the types, and was reinforced when set theory proved to hold a mathematical basis for the whole arrangement.

In 1967, the *Classification Society Bulletin* published an article ('The Pattern of Meaning') in which I put forward the basic scheme of relation codes. To reprint it all here would be wasteful repetition; but its introduction may serve as an alternative presentation of my approach to the subject, and its conclusion may round off the picture.

THE PATTERN OF MEANING

Hitherto, each attempt to make an orderly list of the concepts we use in daily life has been founded on the views of one learned man, or of a group of learned men, as to where each idea may best be fitted into the pattern. However judiciously made, these arrangements are essentially subjective: they are collections of decisions with which we may not always agree. For example, there seems no compelling reason for the social sciences to precede mathematics in the Universal Decimal Classification, nor for the idea of Camembert cheese to appear (as it does, in the revised Roget's Thesaurus) under the heading 'Space: motion with reference to direction'. By and large — give a little and take a little — we know what we mean by the social sciences or Camembert cheese; but that knowledge gives us no clue as to where we may find these concepts in a classification or a thesaurus. For this, we must look in the guide or index to the work. It would be pleasant if, instead, we could tell where an idea should be found merely by considering it in itself, armed with nothing more than a knowledge of its properties. Such a process would place ideas much as the periodic table places the chemical elements: they would hold their positions because, given the rules, they could hold no others.

The periodic table provides a hint as to how we might set about finding a pattern of this type. It arranges the elements according to the structures of the atoms which compose them — structures which determine the behaviour of the atoms, including the behaviour which first suggested the arrangement of the table to Newlands and Mendeleev. A sequence of ideas which is based in some way upon structure may enable us to understand them better, to see why they act as they do, to predict this behaviour, and — if there are gaps in the pattern — to hazard a guess as to which types of idea may one day be found.

INTEGRATIVE LEVELS

The simplest way to apply this principle is to consider the obvious, ordinary things of the world around us. Houses are made of bricks: trees have a trunk each, together with branches and leaves; a chair has legs, a seat and a back; a bicycle has wheels and handlebars. The method may be extended — houses, factories, roads, offices, help to form a town; towns, rivers, hills, fields, valleys make a county, a region, a nation entire. Towards the minuscule, flowers are made of cells, the cells contain plastids, the plastids in their turn have a complicated structure. These observations lead us to a rule which may be helpful: ideas are to be placed after those which form them and before those which they form. A brief examination of the textbooks then produces a sequence of the following sort: particles — atoms — molecules — organelles — cells — organs of the body — people — communities — nations. Side-chains branch out from this arrangement and then rejoin it: some cells form animals other than human, some are embodied in plants, and yet the community known as a farm subsumes all these and so returns them to the main series at a more complex level. Another side-chain, it seems, begins earlier: molecules may form non-living substances and so precede a series of artefacts, single-piece parts which may be brought together to make hand tools, prime movers, power houses, aircraft. Again these may return to the main series at the level of a community: a farm, for example, includes its tractors and its combine harvesters.

This approach appears that of a specialist in naivety; but courage may be taken from those who have already followed the course. These pioneers have given the name 'integrative levels' to the degrees of complexity in the build-up of the world. It seems worth enquiring, is there a special type of idea which acts as a major stage in this build-up? Can we, for instance, choose a few things which appear to mark important steps, places of provisional completion in the sequence? If so, can we find in them any special properties which make them appropriate to these places? If we find such ideas, we may call them the units of the levels they occupy. Indeed, we may name the levels by reference to these types of unit.

Being self-centred, we may take living beings (plants and animals, but especially people) as defining a level, and examine them from a mechanic's point of view. We see that they consist of many interacting systems which keep them in balance with their surroundings, enabling them to persist even in conditions of moderate adversity, to heal themselves if not too badly injured, and generally to resist for a while the ravages of time. This may also be a doctor's or a biologist's viewpoint, though to many it would seem to miss out the desires, interests, emotions, habits and skills which make each person, and even each less advanced animal, different from the rest. This property of stability, thought of as a process of continuous feedback of information allowing self-righting mechanisms to come into play, has been christened homeostasis. Where else may it be found?

It is trite in the studies of history and the social sciences to remark on the self-perpetuating property of communities. Every member of a Trade Union may, in due course, leave that body and be succeeded by a newcomer; an industrial or commercial company may retain its identity — and boast of it — after three hundred years of existence; churches, colleges, societies of all types display this effect. When they are highly organized, specialised systems can be discerned within them: an industrial company has its production system, its personnel system, its internal flow of information leading to its control centres and away from them, its purchasing and sales organs, its maintenance departments. If these all function well, it maintains and even improves its place in the economy.

Below the human being, the other types of animal and the plant, the living cell may be thought of as having self-balancing properties. Offered a proper nutrient medium, it keeps going. Making adjustments in thought to cater for the lower level of complexity, and glossing over months of pondering in a brief sentence, the next object to be taken as meeting our requirements is the molecule. Curiously, atoms (except those of inert gases) do not seem to qualify; the exceptions appear to act as single-atom molecules, just as at higher levels there are single-cell animals and one-man companies. Below the molecule, the sub-atomic particle fits the specification: electrons and protons, the simplest of these (even though they, too, may prove to have a substructure) perform miracles of longevity.

It is arguable whether we may ask what photons are made of, in the same sense that we may ask what a house is made of; but it is possible to describe them and their behaviour in highly sophisticated ways, and the description uses the concepts of mathematics. The essential mass and solidity we associate with most of the things of higher levels has vanished here; but ideas of shape, distribution in space and the like remain. We may think of them as the ideas of geometry. The rule, that concepts fit after the concepts which form them, may now be interpreted to mean that they fit after the concepts we need in order to speak of them. A sequence of ideas used in mathematics is required, which may be expected to end at the advanced point where the ideas of subatomic physics, gravity and the rest begin.

This throws the enquiry back to a study of the basis of mathematics. In due course the idea of shape vanishes in the same way that the idea of mass took its flight, and leaves us with the abstractions of set theory as our sole remaining companions. We reach the set with only one member. Then we reach the empty set. Then we·stop.

Gingerly, we may conclude that there are two more integrative levels here — one of geometry taken as concerned with space, and one of set theory. The levels now total eight: the set-theoretic, the geometric, the sub-atomic and the molecular followed by that concerned with cells, that concerned with plants and animals, that concerned with communities and that concerned with nations. These group themselves neatly in pairs, two of which are the province of logic and mathematics, two are concerned with physics and chemistry, two with the life sciences and two with the social sciences. The arrival of living things appears exactly in the middle of the sequence.

[The article then introduces and explains the principle of relation codes, and concludes as follows] :

To present evidence of a repetitive, teachable pattern in the concepts of daily life is only the start of a programme of research, not its conclusion. A good deal more is known about the holotheme than has been described in this paper — to choose at random, systems of notation have been worked out, based on eight digits, to reduce the relation codes to manageable proportions. Studies of the placing of ideas in complicated fields of work, such as industrial management, have been undertaken. Relation tables have been assembled, and the concepts of number theory — rings, groups, fields and the like — have been put alongside the formative stages of the lowest integrative level. Considerably more specialised terminology than is used here has been adopted. Yet all this, and more besides, remains a fleabite in comparison with the effort still to be made.

What value may be gained from such an effort? A good deal, certainly, and much of it in ways which have not yet become clear. An example of the value it is already known to possess may be taken from the field of co-ordinate indexing, from which the impulse to the present study arose.

Co-ordinate indexing is one of the responses to the current

information explosion. By it, a librarian means a method of bringing together any number of independent ideas which, separately or in concord, describe the subject matter of a document. Usually, but not invariably, he also implies that the ideas are represented by punched feature cards, one card per concept of subject matter, each card bearing up to ten thousand numbered positions representing documents. To stack — say — five cards is to co-ordinate five concepts. The documents which have the five features in common appear in the form of holes which pass through the stack in the relevant numbered positions. This method of search is extremely quick and flexible (and of interest to the statistician also, for the density of holes in the cards is a measure of the likelihood that a document or other item will possess the feature concerned). On the other hand, it is affected by the way the concepts can join themselves together: by problems concerned with homonyms, synonyms, multiple items, separation of monadic terms, and the like. Its efficiency is also dependent on the order in which the cards which represent the concepts are stored. Here, the study of the pattern of meaning has much to contribute. The proper classification of ideas brings synonyms together, separates homonyms, shows which terms are monadic, provides a storage order.

In other directions, if the pattern here developed holds good, effects may be felt in the field of education, in the shaping of general textbooks on science, in the presentation of the relations between subjects in the curricula developed in secondary schools. In the wilder flights of fancy, it is possible to imagine the pattern guiding research in places where little is known. The realm between the quantum of energy and the subatomic particle is not yet well illuminated. The pattern hints at assemblies, systems, combines (whatever these may be at that integrative level) between the two. Will something like this be discovered?

In this case, perhaps we had better wait and see.

Appendix D

SUMMARY OF THE RELATION CODE

The holotheme is divided into two perception classes:
  0 : mundane, containing notions commonly agreed to correspond to reality, such as 'chair', 'man', 'tall', 'green', 'sunshine', 'rain'.
  1 : special, containing notions which are matters of faith, hypothesis or fiction, such as 'Paradise', 'phlogiston', 'Oliver Twist'.

Each class is divided into two kingdoms:
  0 : inanimate, divided into two domains:
    0 : mathematics, divided into two integrative levels:
      0 : set-theoretic
      1 : spatial
    1 : physical sciences, divided into two integrative levels:
      0 : subatomic
      1 : molecular
  1 : animate, divided into two domains:
    0 : life sciences, divided into two integrative levels:
      0 : cytomechanic
      1 : biomorphic
    1 : social sciences, divided into two integrative levels:
      0 : communal
      1 : national

Each integrative level is divided into two ranks:

0 : lower, concerned with notions found within the main units found in the level (for example, within molecules, within animals)

1 : upper, concerned with notions found between the main units found in the level (for example, between molecules, between animals)

Each rank is divided into two groups:
    0 : intransitive, divided into two stages:
        0 : non-symmetric, divided into two formative grades:
            0 : irreflexive (for example, units)
            1 : reflexive (for example, simples)
        1 : symmetric, divided into two formative grades:
            0 : irreflexive (for example, assemblies)
            1 : reflexive (for example, mixtures)
    1 : transitive, divided into two stages:
        0 : non-symmatric, divided into two formative grades:
            0 : irreflexive (for example, series)
            1 : reflexive (for example, sheets)
        1 : symmetric, divided into two formative grades:
            0 : irreflexive (for example, systems)
            1 : reflexive (for example, stretches)

Each formative grade is divided into two varieties:
    0 : passive, divided into two sorts:
        0 : attributive, divided into two semantic types:
            0 : relations (states)
            1 : terms (qualities)
        1 : entitive, divided into two semantic types:
            0 : relations (structures)
            1 : terms (things)
    1 : active, divided into two sorts:
        0 : attributive, divided into two semantic types:
            0 : relations (actions)
            1 : terms (modes)
        1 : entitive, divided into two semantic types:

0 : relations (activities)
1 : terms (phenomena)

The complete pattern is summarized as consisting of two classes, each of eight levels, each of two ranks, each of eight grades, each of eight types.

GENERAL INDEX

This index contains very few references to the placing of specific ideas: for these, the reader should refer to the placement index which follows.

actions : defined 34; their code sequence 35

active ideas : introduced 32; and system theory 75

activities : defined 34; noted 109

adjectives : related to qualities and modes 33; and integrative levels 92; and the holotheme 95

aggregative levels : described 68; mentioned 74; compared with the relation code treatment of substances 71, 72

algebra: and the representation of geometry 55

Anaximander: and constructive order 78

Anaximenes : and constructive order 78

Aristotle : and constructive order 80

artefacts : their integrative level 29, 30

assemblies : as a variety of idea, 25; their code sequence 28, 31

associative property : of relations, 47; referred to the dissociative property (which see), 47.

astrophysics : in the holotheme 72

attributive ideas : introduced 32

Austen, D. : on the theory of integrative levels 74

Bacon, R. : and the position of mathematics in the holotheme 81

Bertalanffy, L. von : and general system theory 75

binary notation : mentioned 14; for perception classes 18; for integrative levels 24, 30; for formative ranks, 31; 32; for formative grades 28, 31, 32, 54; for semantic types 35; for full code sequences 37; for relations in set and number theory 42, 43, 48, 50, 51

binary pattern : in the holotheme 22, 23, 24; and integrative levels 22, 24; and unit ideas 22; and formative grades 28, 54; its validity 59; its nested structure 63, 83

Burnet, J. : on Zeno's doctrine of zero 79

chains of ideas : initial chains, displayed 19, 20, 29; and integrative levels 21, 22, 23, 24, 30, 111; and formative grades and ranks 28, 31, 54; and semantic types 35; and relations 43, 48, 50, 51, 54; and the Elizabethan scheme (Great Chain of Being) 81; in Roget's

PLACEMENT INDEX

This index contains ideas whose position in the holotheme is discussed in the text. It does not contain other notions used in the discussion: for these the reader should refer to the general index.

In deciding whether to admit an idea to the placement index, the rule has generally been to do so even if the idea is only a passing example and is not treated in any depth. The question has been simply, 'Does something in the text relate this notion to others?' If this test has been passed, only excessive triteness or repetition have barred a notion's entry. Thus the notion of wheels does not appear, since the text, in discussing a constructive pattern, provides only the information that they are parts of bicycles. The notion of bicycles appears, however, though not referred to page 111 where the wheels are mentioned. The reference is to page 30, where an explanation is given for the concept appearing in the domain of the life sciences. As to repetition: the notion of an atom is not referred to page 111, although it appears there in a constructive chain. The reason is that the same information is given on page 21, to which the reader is directed.